Taking
INITIATIVES

INITIATIVES *Teacher's Book*

David Curtis

Thomas Nelson and Sons Ltd
Nelson House   Mayfield Road
Walton-on-Thames   Surrey
KT12 5PL   UK

51 York Place
Edinburgh
EH1 3JD   UK

Thomas Nelson (Hong Kong) Ltd
Toppan Building 10/F
22A Westlands Road
Quarry Bay   Hong Kong

Thomas Nelson Australia
480 La Trobe Street
Melbourne   Victoria 3000
Australia

Nelson Canada
1120 Birchmount Road
Scarborough   Ontario
M1K 5G4   Canada

First published by Thomas Nelson and Sons Ltd 1990

ISBN 0-17-432247-X
NPN 9 8 7 6 5 4 3 2 1

Printed in Hong Kong

CONTENTS

INTRODUCTION

Most teachers would probably agree that students learn most effectively under the following conditions:
- they are happy in themselves;
- they experience stability and receive support at home;
- the work they are doing is perceived as purposeful and relevant;
- they are able to make connections with the wider school curriculum and the world beyond school;
- relationships with their teachers and their peers are cooperative and supportive;
- they are able to make discoveries;
- they have some degree of choice and control over what they are doing;
- their classroom environment is pleasant and stimulating;
- they can expect success.

It is obviously very rare for all these conditions to coincide. Every student is different, every teacher will have her own skills and perspective, every classroom has its own specific problems. The learning environment is a matrix of these elements.

Initiatives is designed to contribute to that learning environment in a way that meets as many of the above conditions as possible. The team of nine authors have all written on themes for which they have a particular enthusiasm and classroom experience. Their material is authentic and challenging, their approach student-centred, their focus English in use.

Stress is given to the inter-relationship of whole class and small group work. As well as the four Resourcebooks there are five Investigation Units which are intended for groups of students to use with some independence from their teacher; the students' own research is a central part of every Unit.

All these books have a corresponding set of repromasters to provide the students with further ideas and advice, and there is a tape of related storytelling, songs or discussion on language matters, by a variety of professionals and students, for each of the Resourcebooks.

How this material is used is entirely up to the class teacher. It is envisaged that the Resourcebooks (and their tapes and repromasters) be used by the whole class and that the Investigation Units (and their repromasters) by small

4

groups of up to six students. One way of using *Initiatives* might be for the teacher to work with the whole class using units from the Resourcebooks, setting up a range of optional activities as they occur in the text, until it seems opportune for a group of students to begin more independent work on the appropriate Investigation Unit. But if the teacher, or the students, wishes, small groups can work from Resourcebooks and, just as easily, the whole class can use an Investigation Unit: each of the units in the *Initiatives* books is designed to give a balanced programme of study.

Initiatives is not like a conventional, sequential coursebook. Instead it acknowledges the need for teachers to select material in a way that is most appropriate to their individual students. The options offered can be closely directed by the teacher; alternatively there is the opportunity for negotiation and choice to be part of the learning process. There is a wealth of material here to be seized upon, as the teacher, or the student, sees fit.

Taking Initiatives focuses on these conditions for learning, too. The first part describes twenty aspects of classroom practice, drawing attention to *Initiatives* material as appropriate, then provides a commentary of practical advice and further ideas on each book in turn. Part II tries to give an overview of the contemporary English classroom. Although many of the issues raised may well be familiar, the context of student-centred learning in which they are set is intended to give them greater coherence and weight.

Initiatives has been designed to generate and support coursework for both Standard Grade and GCSE, which share the same principles and aims in relation to the study of English Language. Where *Taking Initiatives* makes reference to GCSE, Standard Grade has not been specifically mentioned too, primarily for the sake of clarity and ease of expression. It may however be useful to Scottish readers to be reminded that years 10 and 11 correspond to S3 and S4. Where additional information regarding the Scottish system is required, as in Chapter 7 of Part II of this book, it is given.

Finally, throughout this book, again for ease of expression, I have referred to a single student as he and to an adult as she. No more should be read into it than that!

PART I

The approach described in *Initiatives* is based on learning through investigation and collaboration. Every opportunity is given for students to work together, at the outset, in the composition and at the culmination of a piece of work; and you are encouraged to organise class discussions, group work with a group varying in size from eight to three, and a great deal of paired work. Students will not necessarily stay in the same group for the whole session. There can be individuals and pairs of students peeling off from larger groups for research or discussion, one group joining another to hold a meeting or compare notes, and students reporting back to the re-assembled class. Because there is the opportunity for choice, there could be different group activities going on at the same time: for example, a group of six might be working from an Investigation Unit and the rest of the class might be engaged in one or more activities taken from *Roots & Routes*. Groups might report their findings to the full class at the end of the session.

Such an approach will greatly benefit the student who can be challenged and stimulated by a combination of good material, an interactive learning method and an imaginative teacher. But these various student groupings all require appropriate furniture arrangements if they are to be productive: a class discussion requires that all the students are able to face each other; group work requires an inward focus and a common work surface; pairs need a degree of isolation. Students need space to move about the classroom without hindrance or causing disturbance to others, and the flexibility to form a temporary working partnership with any member of the class.

But you don't want to be spending eight minutes every session shoving tables and chairs around the classroom. You need an arrangement that requires the minimum of adjustment from session to session and one that can be re-organised very easily and with the minimum of disruption by the students themselves. You will want to experiment constantly with the layout of your room, but the conditions you need can perhaps best be met by the arrangement that is described in Part II, Chapter One of this book where the tables form a work surface around the edge and the chairs form a circle in the middle of the room.

Each session might begin and end with all the class facing inward, seated in this circle. Such a routine would not only give you the chance at the beginning to set up the work clearly and sort out any problems and at the end enable students to share whatever thay have finished; it would also give a very distinct frame to the session, which would be one of your means of establishing the orderliness without which it would be hard to achieve the concentration necessary for learning. You could allow different activities to take place together, and students to work at different rates and on activities requiring short or long periods of time, without losing a tightness of structure. And this structure would then free you for your most valuable teacherly function, that of working alongside your students who are extending and exploring their language.

Resources

The first chapter in Part II of this book goes into detail about the resources you need to build up in your classroom. As well as saving time for your students by having to hand the materials that you can foresee they may need, well-organised and displayed resources will give your room the sort of appearance and feel that will stimulate language study. Books, repromasters, video and audio tapes should be in their place and easily accessible to those students who need to use them.

Tape recorders are in constant use in *Initiatives*, not only for the playing of tapes to full classes and small groups but also for the recording of group discussions, role play activities and interviews in and out of the school. It is vital, then, that your equipment is high quality and robust. Your microphones should be sensitive, unobtrusive but strongly built; and because they will inevitably break down with distressing frequency you will need a speedy and efficient repair system.

You will almost certainly want to supplement whatever work you are doing from *Initiatives* with your own resources. This might mean supporting a unit of work with a collection of material that would serve as a background display. If, for example, you were doing work that involved the study of the daily press from *On and Off the Record* (The Man in the Crate, 70-74), or, with a small group, from *Campaign* (Handling the Press, pages 30-32) you might have as a backdrop to the work a wide range of one day's newspapers; if you were working from Unit 5 of *The Right Idea* (pages 99-100) you might use a display like this to provide material out of which students could create 'found poems'.

If you are working with some of the units in *Initiatives* you might want to set up a display of books from the school or local library which could be used by students to extend their reading of the subject. Work on names from Unit 1 of *Roots & Routes* might prompt you to collect a small selection of texts on derivation. You might want to support your work on Christopher Nolan (pages 30-32 of the same book) with all his published works. *Other Worlds* might prompt a big display, or an injection into the school library of science fiction books. Work on Dick Turpin, Marilyn Monroe and Winnie Mandela (from Unit 2 of *On and Off the Record*) might give rise not only to additional material about these characters but also to books about others you might wish your students to have the opportunity to study as well or instead.

Control

I watched a teacher from the back of the classroom last week trying to cope with a particularly awkward tenth year student, and discussing the problem afterwards I could not come up with a solution to it. Management of students is one of the most intractable, demanding and complex issues you have to face, and although topical, worthwhile and attractively presented material and involving classroom strategies will help enormously, there will still be difficult students like the boy above who will continually stretch all your resources. It may be possible to do a containing job which enables the rest of the class to get on for most of the time with their work, but this is not really satisfactory, for the student who lacks self-discipline or for the rest of the class. In any case, your aim has to be the creation of a classroom atmosphere that is supportive and tolerant of every student's attempt at learning. The Headteacher who sent his sensitive son to another school because his own was too rough was not recognising that it was his responsibility to create a learning environment in which students of all types were able to flourish.

An attempt is made to deal with indiscipline in Part II, Chapter Five of this book. There have to be some ground rules, worked out between yourself and your students and applied to behaviour in and around the classroom, in small group work and in plenary activities. Each student needs to know what is expected of him and how dependent the success and satisfaction of his classmates are on him. The importance of mutual respect, between students and between the students and the teacher, is implicit throughout *Initiatives* and in its themes and approaches to learning and should be made explicit when misbehaviour becomes disruptive. A session devoted to discussion on the interdependence of the members of a class and the value of a mutually supportive community might occasionally be necessary.

You and your department should rely on talk as the means by which the understanding that underlies good behaviour can be gained. You might have to give a great deal of time to talk, much of it one-to-one, before you make any headway with difficult students. And you will also have to have in the background clearly understood sanctions which you can fall back on should you need to; but these too should be based on the principle that talk must be the main strategy.

You cannot develop the research work described in *Initiatives* with individuals and small groups leaving the classroom, perhaps leaving the school grounds, unless your students have achieved a considerable degree of self discipline. The catch, of course, is that self-discipline will develop out of investigative work because it is so rewarding. You will have to take the odd risk, hoping that less reliable students will behave responsibly; if they don't they will have to forfeit the chance of working in this way for a while. When they have shown some sign that they might be trusted they will be allowed to try again.

It is a very delicate balance. But there is no point at all, if you are interested in developing mature, independent learners, in running your classroom like a barracks. You have to be ready to trust your students and have to build up their trust in you by ensuring that you are always sensitive to their individual needs.

Choice

One of the principles underlying *Initiatives* is that students should be given scope to make their own choices in English sessions. This principle recognises that every class is made up of individuals, each with his own propensities and inclinations, enthusiasms and skills, and acknowledges that true learning requires a commitment that can only be given if the student feels involved in the activity from the outset. It is the degree to which you take this principle of choice that has to be thought through.

In each section of work in *Initiatives* there are lists of options, usually in sets of four. Students will be encouraged to make their selection, and you would probably ensure that all options were taken up. There is also the work in Investigation Units which might be available to a group on request. And beyond that is the possibility for a student or a group to continue studies beyond the material or the assignments offered in either the Resourcebook   or the Investigation Units.

As their teacher you will need to ensure that every student
•has a balanced English curriculum, in other words that he spends an appropriate time engaged in a range of speaking and listening, reading and writing activities;
•has the opportunity to make contexts within which he can not only build on those skills he already has proficiency in but also work at those in which he is less successful;
•is meeting the statements of attainment of the National Curriculum.

As their teacher you will need to
•know each student well enough to judge how much scope he can manage and when to allow him to experience more;
•know what sort of work he would be inclined to neglect that he should be doing from time to time;
•ensure that when there are four options on offer each is taken up by one group or another so that the processes and the results can be shared by the class as a whole.

If students are to be doing a variety of different activities in their classroom, you will need to give them the opportunity to share their work with each other. Then all can learn from the experiences of their classmates and

11

all are more able to exercise choice sensibly because they are becoming more informed about the nature and satisfactions of an increasing range of activities.

You would need to be involved in real negotiation, in which you try to balance the needs of the student as perceived by himself and by you, and take into account how capable he is of taking advantage of some freedom of choice: the very act of negotiation, with its building of compromise out of broadening insights through a careful use of language, is integral to the English experience.

The Real Thing

Most of us know real ale when we drink it and real reading when we do it, but what of real English? Let's start with what it isn't. Real English is not exercises. It is not those exercises that are intended to test a student's powers of comprehension, come in the form of lists of questions after a passage of prose or a poem and require regurgitated factual information. It is not teacher's spelling lists or teacher's activities for learning how to use a semi-colon. It is not an assignment for the student to describe a day in the life of a penny or describe the sunset or even write an essay about the importance of democracy – unless the student has been given a context which makes the activity meaningful to him, or unless he himself has chosen to do it.

Real English is work on the English language that has genuine meaning for the student.

This meaningfulness might be achieved if the work has
•context: in *Initiatives* the context is provided by the language focus of the four Resourcebook and the five Investigation Units and by their subject matter.
•function: there is always a reason for the student to do the work. There is a purpose behind it, like in *Roots & Routes* (page 10) when a student can choose to keep a language diary for a week, compare it with a partner's and share his thoughts with the rest of the class.
•a national, local or topical significance: as in *On and Off the Record* where students are invited to explore the treatment given to the Umaru Dikko 'Man in the Crate' story by the media.
•an authentic imaginative power: as in *The Right Idea* (page 33) when students can improvise two scenes based

on characters identified in a wedding photograph, set before the ceremony takes place and later at the reception.
•a potential for genuine study: as in *Comedy &Humour* where there is an opportunity to gain an insight into the nature of laughter.

And it can be enhanced by the teacher's classroom approach. She can give a study more reality by the use of local experts, as in *Opening Up the Airwaves* when journalists employed by the regional press can be invited in; she can encourage research into the dialects of peers and teachers in *Roots & Routes* (page 76) or find a different audience by giving a group's completed *Campaign* presentation to students from another school or to parents at an open evening.

Out of Classroom

You might have the space to make a quiet area in a corner of your room out of bookshelves or a screen in which a small group of students could read or write or work with a tape recorder. It might provide those using it with a degree of seclusion. Should you be lucky enough to have access to a space, an empty room or a walk-in cupboard near your classroom, you could use that instead or as well.

If you have one or more groups involved in activities like role play which are inevitably noisy, a space outside the classroom would be invaluable. Sometimes a group will leave the classroom to develop an improvisation in the school grounds; sometimes a performance will be given to students in another classroom.

Students working with Investigation Units might be leaving the classroom to gather information, from the school library, from another classroom, from other students or members of staff. They might, during lesson time
•do research in the library (*Opening up the Airwaves*, page 34, producing a radio documentary);
•conduct surveys in the school (*Comedy & Humour*, page 7, What different ages laugh at);
•hold interviews with other students (*Other Worlds*, page 9, views on science fiction);
•hold interviews with teachers (*Agony Column*, page 11, on Attitudes to Agony Aunts);

13

• present their findings to students in another classroom (*Campaign*, page 41, planning the presentation).

Increasingly, pupils in primary school are involved in work that has an explicit purpose and are encouraged to work independently of their teacher. Increasingly, they are becoming used to taking choices, reflecting on their progress, having responsibility for what they do. You will expect a more responsible and self-disciplined attitude to grow steadily with the years as these students arrive at and move through secondary school.

Not that having students moving in and out of the classroom will ever be anything other than hazardous! To ensure that problems are kept to a minimum, you will need to
• feel confident that the students are genuinely involved in the work;
• have built up a classroom ethos of mutual trust and high morale;
• have an agreed code of behaviour;
• have a tight system of sanctions, understood by all the students and enforced when necessary;
• have a very simple permission slip for students leaving the classroom;
• allow out at first only those in whom you have complete (or nearly complete) confidence;
• make explicit that such scope brings its own intrinsic satisfactions;
• gradually allow others to go, probably paired with students who have already shown they can sustain independent study;
• be prepared to curtail the movements of a student until you feel you can trust him.

And if you do not feel you can rely on the good behaviour of your students beyond the classroom, don't let them go. None of the work requires them to leave the classroom. All the essential material is provided within the Resourcebooks, even within the Investigation Units. If you do wish them to carry out research but do not wish them to leave the classroom during lesson time, they can do it at break or after school for homework.

Field Work

For the study of English to be properly investigative it

14

is vital for students to break free of a book and classroom-bound education. An enormous amount of genuine exploration of the language can take place through interviews and surveys conducted within the school, and the subject can be brought vividly to life in this way. But just beyond the school gates a wealth of language activity is taking place:

•On page 45 of *Roots & Routes* in the section headed Giving the Community a Voice, are the options 'How many different influences/languages can you find in your town? Can you find any examples of local dialect on display? Search for graffiti that expresses questions in your area.'

•On page 77 in the section A Manner of Speaking students are invited to 'Generate a piece of research at home'; and

•On page 97 in the section No Dialects Please to 'Conduct a community survey: what do people in your area feel about the use of dialect?'

There are many other examples of such work, in *Roots & Routes*, in the other three Resourcebooks and, as you would expect, in the Investigation Units. Students are invited to broaden their studies by visiting the local community with a tape recorder, the local theatre to watch a play, the town library to access bigger information banks than the school carries, or the local television or radio station or the press to see at first-hand how the media work.

This sort of activity is bound to enliven the subject for the students and alert them to their language environment. It is real investigation. Those students going out on such a project and those waiting to hear the outcome will be involved in genuine research, and the more thoroughly it is prepared for, the more genuine it will become. The purpose will have to be clarified, plans will have to be properly made, interviews trialled, samples of the populace carefully chosen and equipment checked.

As well as all this, a decision will have to be made as to whether or not the group will be accompanied by a member of staff, a teacher who is not teaching at that time, an ancillary member of staff or a curriculum support teacher from TVE or an LEA team. If students are going to be leaving the school premises during lesson time it is essential that a letter is sent home asking permission from parents, and the Headteacher will have to agree. But you would not be able to allow your students to work in this way if you had any doubts about their commitment to the work. A bad experience in the town would set back such activities for a long time.

All the research in *Initiatives* that requires out-of-school work is optional. If you feel that your students should not be operating so far from your own supervision during lesson time you should not allow them to choose such an activity. You may have students you do not yet altogether trust to work in this way without mishap. These students might be asked to conduct research for homework, in the evenings or over the weekend, and if this is done satisfactorily you might consider letting them do their next survey during the school day.

Homework

In *Several Stories High* the unit The Story of Your Family (page 118) has a section on research into family history. Students are asked to find out where their families come from, what occupations their forefathers and mothers had, whether they had any particularly outstanding ancestors and, if so, what they were like. The material uncovered might inspire a story. In *Roots & Routes* (page 12), The Language of Life, are the options 'Talk to your family about your family history. Get them to go as far back in time as they can ' and 'Listen to or tape anecdotes from older relatives'. And on page 32 of *The Right Idea* students are encouraged to hunt out old family photograph albums and select some interesting snaps.

These homeworks are set out explicitly in *Initiatives* but there are occasions throughout the books when you might decide to set homework of a similar sort. In *On and Off the Record* (page 45), for example, you might ask students to research the work of the carpenter, social worker or landscape gardener that they will play in role later for class work.

The strength of homework assignments like these is
• they spring from the context of ongoing classwork;
• they involve genuine research into language and media

16

matters;
- they involve people from the family and the community as experts;
- they encourage a greater understanding of the family and the community;
- the students' work is largely independent of the teacher;
- the material gathered will be of value to the rest of the class;
- they can be carried out by students working together in each other's homes or in their community;
- they are fun.

Cross-Curricular Work

Subject boundaries have never really been more than an administrative convenience and experiments in secondary school of integrated days, integrated courses and linking across subjects for particular projects are showing that the advantages to learning of a subject-based approach are outweighed by the disadvantages.

Among the advantages of a cross-curricular approach are that
- teachers from different disciplines working together can quickly find a great deal of common ground;
- teachers planning together can share techniques and generate ideas;
- the students can enjoy work that is student-centred with a clear purpose behind it and a context for the development of particular skills.

The work in *Initiatives* is real work. The assignments are all to do with an exploration of the real world, of literature, of language, of documentary, of the media, and this reality would be heightened by cross-curricular approaches. You might want to encourage students working on a science fiction story from *Other Worlds* to make sure that the material in their story is scientifically accurate; or that they fully understand the implications of the environmental disaster depicted in The Westbridge Incident, the simulation exercise on pages 56-59 of *On and Off the Record*. This may require no more than a chat in the staffroom with a Science teacher so that she can either talk to this group, cover the issue in one of her sessions or give your group the opportunity to conduct some experimentation in her classroom at a convenient time. If the school darkroom is the preserve of the Science department, agreement would have to be reached between you and the teacher with responsibility to enable your students to explore their ideas about photography generated in the early part of *On and Off the Record* (pages 10-13) and *The Right Idea* (page 12). This sort of tentative collaboration across subject boundaries would be very beneficial to students, who would be able to take their interests a stage further.

For the processes in *Initiatives* to have real significance it is crucial that the products are of a high quality. Students are invited in *Agony Column* to produce brochures on a subject that concerns them; similarly, to write a protest leaflet in *Roots & Routes* (page 121); in *Opening up the Airwaves* to make a jingle announcing the radio station and in *The Right Idea* to present a report based on a *Which?* test. If such products are to be of high standard, collaboration with the Technology department or the Expressive Arts faculty is very important. An agreement with the relevant teacher for a group of your students to work on their assignments from time to time in a corner of her classroom might be sufficient, and it is likely that the teacher, recognising the benefits to her own subject, would be happy for this to happen and perhaps develop.

Out of such minimal collaboration the need for closer curricular links might be identified, leading to attempts to build into the timetable structural ties. If sessions for a year group in English and Expressive Arts or Technology were timetabled consecutively, cross-curricular activity could take place as a matter of course, to the benefit of all concerned.

Cross-Phase

There is an option on page 27 of *Roots & Routes* inviting students to 'write ... an early reading book for children using the 250 most common words'. Unless students choosing this option work from the start very closely with the eventual recipients of their finished book or books they will have missed the chance of getting the full benefit of this activity. They should visit the primary school, having taken the responsibility of making the arrangements themselves. They should have a discussion about the characteristics and qualities of such books with the teacher responsible for English in the primary school, meet some children to get ideas, perhaps the subject for the story, and keep in touch with them during the drafting stages. (They might find Repromaster 28 a useful resource.) On the book's completion they should give a presentation in the primary school.

On page 59 of the same book are further opportunities for productive contact with children from primary school. The options to plan an advertising campaign to 'sell' a punctuation mark and to produce a handbook of punctuation tips and exercises give the chance for purposeful collaboration across the phases, so that younger and older students can learn from each other. And the realness of the task will give extra zest to the project.

You would get more benefit from such collaboration if the primary school in question were a feeder school to your secondary school. Such links should lead to ease of transition for the student moving from one school to the next. Continuity of experience across the primary/ secondary divide has always been desirable; now the National Curriculum requires programmes of study in secondary schools to mesh with those in primary school and for students' records to trace an uninterrupted school career.

To enable mutual understanding and trust to grow across the phases you may wish to
•exchange teachers for short or long periods of time;
•hold regular meetings between the English department and teachers with responsibility for English in your feeder primary schools;
•hold cross-moderation sessions between the English department and teachers from your feeder schools;
•enable students from one phase to visit the other when appropriate;
•take advantage of work like the options described above from *Initiatives* to find real collaboration and real audiences in the feeder primary schools, so that teachers get to know each other in the course of this routine work and students get used to learning from each other across the age gaps.

The Visiting Expert

On one occasion I invited a senior trade union official to come and talk to the class, which he duly did – with little regard for the low boredom threshold of most of us. He concluded that he had given more credibility to the theory that young people cannot listen like they used to; I concluded that next time I would brief the visiting expert more carefully in the technique of working with sixteen year-olds. For one thing you recognise the nature of your audience, its possible interests, attitudes and predispositions; for another, you think of ways in which it may be helped to become involved.

There are opportunities throughout *Initiatives* for experts to be brought into the classroom. You will probably want the students themselves to be responsible for the arrangements, but it would be as well for you to check times and hospitality: the poem *Head of English* in *The Right Idea* (page 19) makes me squirm as I remember incidents in my own classroom sadly not very different from this one. On all occasions in *Initiatives* when an expert from beyond the classroom is suggested, there is a context to the work which should make her contribution pertinent and well-received.

Among the various experts you might welcome into your classroom are:
• the national figure: the author or a storyteller;
• the student or students from another English class with a presentation of work they have been doing;
• the professional from the community: the newspaper journalist, the worker from the paper mills, the television camera operator ...
• the member of the community who has something special and relevant to offer: the first world war veteran, the person with an authentic dialect unusual in the area, the person who has kept a personal journal through changing times ...
• the student from this class who has been involved in some lengthy research or has been asked to find out about something that has cropped up and returns to give his information to the rest.

And you will probably wish to establish a code of behaviour out of discussion with your students for such events: a balance should be struck, for example, between

20

proper, warm respect for the expert and the need to question her closely, though always politely, so that students can follow through arguments as far as they can, learning more about learning and about questioning without giving offence.

Interviewing

One of the means of gathering information recommended in *Initiatives* is conducting surveys, and there are repromasters which offer a possible framework for questioning. Your students will need to think carefully about the purposes behind the survey before they start so that they can devise the most useful questions, and they will need to decide whom to question to give validity to the survey. It might be their intention to ask people from a particular social group or a particular age. They might wish to take people from a particular profession or in a particular role, or they might be looking for two contrasting groups or a cross-section of the community. In any event, they should make sure they have a valid selection of people for interview. A detailed description of the criteria used for determining who would be the subjects for interview might be given as part of the report. It is in the nature of surveys that the questions will be fairly brief and the opportunities for extended follow-up rare, so the questions themselves should be worked on, worded carefully and trialled to make sure they yield the information the students are looking for.

With full-blown interviews the preparation of questions is just as important, and a great deal of research should go into the subject before the event. Even when the interviewee is a student from the same class, as on page 6 of *Roots &Routes*: 'Tape an interview with a partner about their experience of language and how they see their future involvement with language', your student shouldn't launch into his questioning before he has thought through his techniques of interrogation thoroughly.

With a person not met before, preparation is more necessary and should be a longer process. Unless your students follow the kind of routine described on page 45 of *On and Off the Record* they will not get the best out of their subject. I was recently sent a tape of my uncle being interviewed for Devon radio on his experience of spending a lifetime in a small rural community. He did very well, but his breathlessness, caused by the tensions of the interview itself, forced him to give short answers and rendered his contribution bereft of the anecdotes I have heard him enjoy telling in easier circumstances, and which would have given the interviewer the colour and drama he was looking for. Your students will need to find ways to relax their subject, and the advice that Tony Parker gives, which is summarised on page 131of *On and Off the Record*, is extremely helpful. Detailed advice on interviewing can be found on Repromasters 1a, 1b, 2a, 2b and 3 of *Other Worlds* and Repromaster 11 of *Opening Up the Airwaves*.

Also of help in the management of the interview itself might be the section in *Agony Column* headed Getting the Cat out of the Bag, an option inviting students to investigate the methods of well-known interviewers. Practical tips on the complex business of preparing the subject, putting him at ease, freeing his mind and his tongue and following through a theme might be picked up during this analysis. Your students will also need to concentrate on developing the skills of active listening ...

Role Play and Simulations

Drama ought to exist on the timetable as a subject in its own right and it ought to appear across the curriculum as an important strategy for learning. And now that NCC has placed drama in the English domain it is right that it should be fully integrated and implemented within that subject. In the *Initiatives* books drama as whole class, group and paired activities is routine.

The full class improvisations that are suggested should not be daunting, but you will need to establish certain conventions. You will need, for example, to ensure that when you want your students to freeze in silence they will do that. A sharp clap might be your signal. You might like to use a few simple warm-up exercises before starting a session, serving the purposes of loosening up mentally and physically and also of creating from the beginning a sense of creative concentration.

With the full class improvisation I should also start by forming students into tableaux; by taking away sound and

22

movement you will be able to make the shape you are looking for. Next you might want to add movement, your students going through the motions of the improvisation using mime. Then you might allow the improvisation to develop into dialogue. The 'busy social life in the courtyard' from page 86 of *Several Stories High* or the 'market trader barking' from page 54 of *The Right Idea* can burst into life, until you clap and establish the silent tableaux again.

Group role play activities and paired work should also be quite manageable in the English classroom, though you will have to ensure that your students learn to talk to each other fairly softly. On page 45 of *Several Stories High* students in groups of six decide on their roles in a soap opera script conference. On page 59 of *On and Off the Record* students in groups of five meet in role as a Committee of Inquiry into the Westbridge chemical disaster. In these two cases and in many more like them the whole class can be divided into small groups doing the same work. You will probably find that the work will generate an intense involvement, students will speak with hushed urgency, and a great deal of purposeful and effective interaction will take place.

These group role play activities are relatively static. Where the activity is inevitably going to lead to movement and noise you will have to find ways to safeguard your own mental state and the wellbeing of nearby colleagues by limiting the number of groups involved in that sort of work. If you have access to a small room or space near your classroom, one group could develop an improvisation there. If you have a screen in your classroom or a book corner you might be able to isolate the improvisation to an extent from the other students. I don't think you could satisfactorily accommodate more than one such improvisation in your classroom at any one time, and I don't think it would be fair to your other students doing other work if there were undue and prolonged distractions.

Transcribing a tape

From time to time you may want a pair of students to make a written transcript of an audiotape; I say from time to time because although it can be an extremely worthwhile activity, it is a painfully slow one.

It would be useful before doing any transcriptions to have conventions for the various signifiers your students will need to use, if not throughout the department at least in your class. Agreement over how you will denote a pause, a grunt, more than one person speaking at the same time or indecipherable speech will make the transcript more of a true record than it would otherwise be, and so more useful. There is detailed advice about transcription on Repromaster 3 of *On and Off the Record* and Repromaster 8 of *Several Stories High*.

Because trying to reproduce on paper the precise nature of an oral activity is such a slow process, it is a very good means of studying the language. Firstly the process itself of listening acutely to what is going on throughout the tape and the deciphering and reproduction based on prediction and grammatical deduction will enable the student to focus on language constructions in a very intense way. Then, when the transcript has been written, it provides a text that can be scrutinised for whatever characteristics that form of oral interaction might display. If it is a transcript of small group discussion, the social and linguistic features of the discourse might be looked at; if of an interview, skills of questioning and answering might be considered. An orally told story might be looked at for the features that the spoken language exhibits that are not to be found in the written form. Because the students are working with material for which they themselves have been responsible, in its inception and transcription, they will be inclined to treat it with special attention. The context is made by themselves as investigators.

The third stage might be the use to which the transcript is put as material for a further piece of writing. The small group discussion might become the basis of a discursive piece or a scene in a short story; the interview might be developed into a playscript and the spoken story might be written up as a short story, enabling the investigation into the differences between spoken and written English to be continued.

Journals

In various parts of *Initiatives* students are offered the

option of keeping a journal. The writing over a term of a reading journal is suggested on page 57 of *Several Stories High*. The process here would begin with two students devising a list of questions which they could apply to every book they read and at any stage of the reading. Every time they read they would write down the answers to their questions, by the end of a term have built up a considerable amount of materials and at this stage be able to look back over the period to see how they had developed. A more conventional diary is proposed on page 35 of *The Right Idea*. It would be kept for just a week, after which time the student could choose two extracts, one to become the basis of a polished piece of prose, the other of poetry. And on page 65 of *On and Off the Record* is the suggestion that students might like to use the journal idea to reflect on how their small group has worked, how ideas were generated and how decisions were made.

Although the functions of these three types of journal at first appear to be distinct, they perform a very similar purpose. All three enable the student to express himself as he wishes in a reflective way on matters that are current. He is not creating a product, but instead keeping a note, making a record that is in itself a process helpful to focusing his thoughts. And this record might be used later as material for further work.

The journal as a useful device for classroom management is discussed in Part II of this book. But it is also a means for the development of expressive writing, and as such an instrument for the extension of understanding. I think it should be kept in the loose-leaf folder with all your student's work; but it might contain confidential material and this confidentiality should obviously be respected. It might, then, be kept separate from the other work, and a device to achieve this is the plastic clip-on spine. If your student uses such a spine and gives his journal a front and back cover he can keep it with his other work while establishing that it is different, and he can add and take away from it as he sees fit. Any material that he no longer wants to retain he can pick out; anything that he wants to add – pages from a notebook containing snatches of dialogue heard on a bus, family letters, old photographs – can be clipped in. And a specialist journal only requires another plastic spine.

Drafting

Before you can really put yourself in your students' shoes over a matter like drafting you will need to be a writer yourself. You need to have had experience in using writing to try to find words that will express exactly how you think and feel about an issue. This experience will probably have failed in the sense that words may not quite have achieved that goal, but succeeded in that you will have a clearer picture of your thoughts or feelings and a clearer sense of what words can do: it will have been a learning experience. You really need to have written seriously for audiences outside yourself as well, when the process of shaping your language is determined by its communicative effectiveness and its style.

There are two descriptions of redrafting in *Initiatives*. In Part II of this book the process is described, and illustrated with specific reference to the writing of a poem which is taken through several stages, the result of class collaboration between teacher and student. It is described in detail on pages 26 and 27 of *The Right Idea*, with the author pointing out that we each have to develop our own writing process and offering one model with five distinct stages which he calls Pre-Writing, The First Draft, Revising, Proof-Reading and Publishing (see Repromaster 6).

In these two passages the importance of collaboration is stressed. Generally it will be useful to spend time before any writing in discussion as a class, as a small group or a pair. The sharing of ideas will almost invariably produce more ideas, among them some that might well have remained dormant without the pulse of adrenalin that talk can generate. In most cases, sharing a piece of work with the teacher or a classmate will help develop a clearer sense of the reader's needs; and in most cases, jotting down random ideas, making spider diagrams or listing whatever words come into your head, however vaguely they relate to your theme, is a helpful prelude to more systematic planning. But "we each have to develop our own writing process". There will be students who prefer to work from start to finish on their own, whose redrafting takes the form of attempting to get it right first time. When they fail

26

in the course of this one attempt, they cross out, substitute, rephrase, reorder and arrow. They then rewrite their fair copy out of the hotch-potch. This is probably how many writers work, whether they use a pen, pencil or word processor: through a single process that cannot be broken down into discrete stages.

Students are now recognising that writing generally means redrafting; that it differs from speaking in that the writer has the opportunity to re-shape his meaning before giving it to anyone else. One of the statements of attainment for the English National Curriculum at Level 3 reads
"Begin to revise and redraft in discussion with the teacher, other adults, or other children in the class, paying attention to meaning and clarity as well as checking for matters such as correct and consistent use of tenses and pronouns";
but on each occasion the degree of redrafting will be determined by the nature of the particular piece of writing and by how much time the student wishes to spend on it. As a guide to the sort of questions he should be asking himself at the end of a piece he will find *The Right Idea*, page 112, very useful. The process of editing is detailed on Repromaster 36; work on brainstorming on Repromasters 23 and 24 of the same book, and further drafting activities are to be found on Repromasters 9 and 23 of *Several Stories High*.

A Graffiti Board

Graffiti are an ancient and demotic form of poetic protest. Mention is made of them on page 14 of *On and Off the Record,* where Kilroy's blunt statement and Edwin Morgan's poem on the Channel Tunnel are quoted. The ubiquitous Kilroy crops up again on page 124 of *Roots &Routes* in a section headed The Writing on the Wall, which deals with the nature of graffiti and attitudes to it. On page 48 of *Several Stories High* a graffito is used as an example of a (very) short story. In two other places in this book students have the option of collecting inscriptions from the tombstones of the local graveyard (page 32) and collecting the last lines from novels (page 20). Both these collections could be mounted on a graffiti board, as illustrated on the following page.

Example of Graffiti Board

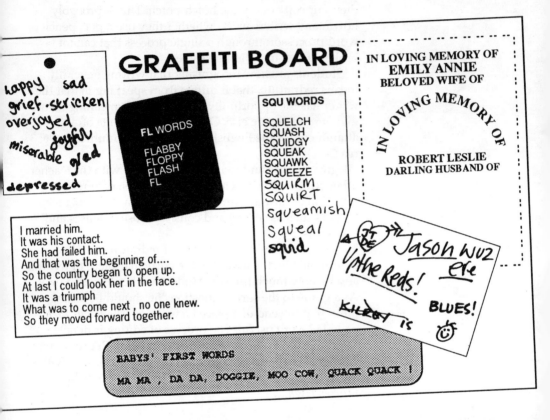

GRAFFITI BOARD

happy   sad
grief-stricken
overjoyed
    joyful
miserable glad

depressed

FL WORDS

FLABBY
FLOPPY
FLASH
FL

SQU WORDS

SQUELCH
SQUASH
SQUIDGY
SQUEAK
SQUAWK
SQUEEZE
SQUIRM
SQUIRT
squeamish
squeal
squid

IN LOVING MEMORY OF
EMILY ANNIE
BELOVED WIFE OF

IN LOVING MEMORY OF

ROBERT LESLIE
DARLING HUSBAND OF

I married him.
It was his contact.
She had failed him.
And that was the beginning of....
So the country began to open up.
At last I could look her in the face.
It was a triumph
What was to come next , no one knew.
So they moved forward together.

Jason wuz
ere
Up the Reds!
BLUES!
KILROY IS

BABYS' FIRST WORDS

MA MA , DA DA, DOGGIE, MOO COW, QUACK QUACK !

You might wish to have a graffiti board permanently in your classroom. Sometimes it might present fairly literary examples of short stories as mentioned on the previous page, but more often might provide an opportunity for students' self-expression on themes of your or their choice. The board might take the form of a large sheet of black paper, or you may be able to provide a brick wall backcloth. If you no longer use your blackboard for teaching, that would serve. You will need to establish from the start what is <u>not</u> acceptable! Used well it could be a rich and changing resource for the study of language.

Grouping

A flick through the *Initiatives* books produces a dozen different activities that students working in pairs or small groups might do:
- editing
- drafting
- interviewing
- role playing/improvising
- planning questions
- preparing for a survey
- comparing experiences
- inventing new words
- selecting material
- ordering material
- reporting back
- preparing a display,

and there are, of course, many more. It would be limiting for their learning experiences if students habitually formed into the same pairs or small groups, so, although you will wish to encourage choice of partners, you will need to negotiate with them to ensure frequent changes. You will want changing combinations to provide
- a mix of boys and girls;
- a contrast in experience;
- a contrast in skills and abilities;
- challenge;
- change;
- stimulus.

To enable students to form readily into different groupings there need to be
- frequent, bracing full class activities, sharing of work and times of reflection;
- an atmosphere of mutual respect, support and collaboration;
- furniture arranged in such a way that students don't have a particular, static, home base.

Teacher Intervention

When you feel the moment is right you will want to focus the student's attention on particular features of language. He will have created a context of narrative, descriptive or expository writing and you will sense that the time is ripe for intervention. To help you in this attempt to move on a student's writing skills by asking the

29

right question or offering a piece of advice you might make a sort of check list or scheme like the one below, which identifies important features of written language.

CHOICE OF WORDS	FLOW	VITALITY
Clarity	Varying lengths of sentences	Metaphor
Simplicity	Links within sentences/ paragraphs	Comparison/ contrast
Connotations	Links between paragraphs	Openings/ middles/ends
Economy of expression	Controlling idea for paragraph/piece	Climax
Emphasis	Rhythms and cadences	Anecdote
Derivation	Natural order in time/ chronological	Personal experience
Sound	Natural order in space/ descriptions of big before small	Concreteness
Familiarity	Clarity of position in time and space	Use of senses
Repetition	Clarity of function of piece	Verb density
Appropriateness	Clear sense of audience	New perspective
Technicality	Tone under control	Paradox
Theme	Mood under control	Revelation
Mot juste	Knowledge of subject	Axiom
Felicitous phrase	Narrative voice	Analogy

Initiatives pays a lot of attention to the language of persuasion. Almost every book contains at least one section which deals with bias. You may want to help your students understand more about the ways in which the same argument can be couched in terms which convey tentativeness or subjectivity, or objective authority. By learning more about the spectrum from 'It makes me mad when I see ... ' through 'It seems to me ... ' to 'Research shows ... ' and 'Fish are ... ', your student can become a more independent reader and a more influential writer.

Well into *The Right Idea*, on page 112, is a section entitled Self-Criticism which aims to direct the student inwards to looking at his recent writing with a cold eye. Has he tried as hard as he could have? Has he spent as much time on it as he should? What would he say about it if someone else had written it? The author is trying to develop a sense of responsibility in the student for the work that he does by urging him to recognise honestly what his attitude has been.

A list of questions at the end of *Agony Column* covers the same ground: how successful have the student's efforts been? Has he communicated what he intended to? Did he find working with a partner useful? By raising the learning process onto a conscious and explicit level the student, reflecting on what he has done, has to confront the question which informs much of the work in *Initiatives*: what have I learnt?

The author of *On and Off the Record* continually turns the student back on himself. On page 45 he asks 'Does it help to have a prepared list of questions – or not? Could the research have been better done?' What has he learnt about the subject under study? What has he learnt about himself as a learner?

You will probably wish to establish a routine at the end of a session or sequence of sessions in which students share their work in progress or their finished product. Sometimes you may organise the materials in *Initiatives* so that three or four activities are done at the same time by groups of students who will present their work at the end. On pages 94 and 95 of *On and Off the Record*, for example, there are instructions for three activities, the compiling of a yearbook, a scrapbook and a minichronicle. If your students each choose to do one of these and on finishing the task present their books to the rest, the act of presentation itself will teach them about what they have done and how well they have done it, and it will inform the remainder of the class. If the presentation is followed by a sensitive evaluation of the quality of the product there is the additional opportunity for all to benefit.

The same routine should apply to drama presentations. After the performance there should be a lengthy time given to critical evaluation. Out of a frank, delicate (and increasingly informed) exchange of views will grow the understanding that will result in work of a higher quality next time.

Language and Learning

You might find the diagram opposite useful. It is intended to show the importance of context to a specific task, how that task is influenced in the doing by the nature of the product, and the processes of language involved. It is meant to represent learning across the curriculum, not only in English. The questions are meant to be answered by you – the teacher.

Presentation and Display

It will be clear from these notes that the work in *Initiatives* is real English: the issues are significant, the investigations genuine; the information and understanding gained are worthwhile.

The products of this work are various – essays, graphs, collages, letters, pamphlets, videotapes, audiotapes, research papers, plays. Some of them will have a real audience well beyond the school. The letter written to an author will be delivered – we hope – to her. The rest should be presented, in a way that is appropriate to each piece, within the community in which the school is set or within the school itself.

You may want to round off each session with a presentation of work in progress and completed work. Such a routine would provide an ongoing audience for your students' work and a means by which response, criticism and acclaim could foster self-respect, self-evaluation, an interplay of ideas and tasks and a development of skills. And you may wish to ensure that

32

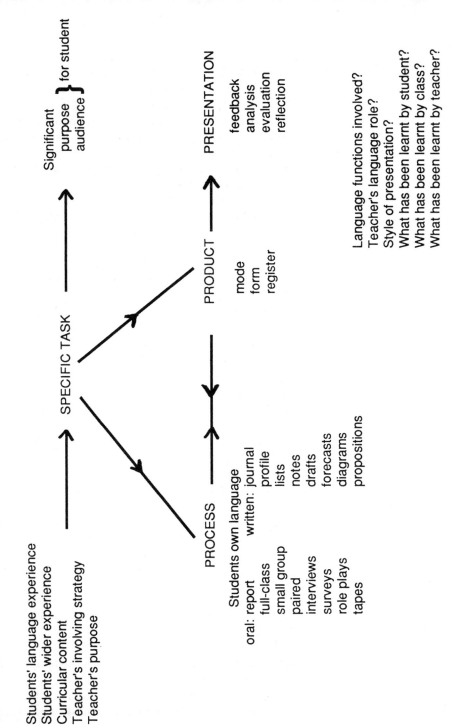

LANGUAGE AND LEARNING

Students' language experience
Students' wider experience
Curricular content
Teacher's involving strategy
Teacher's purpose

Significant
purpose ⎱ for student
audience ⎰

SPECIFIC TASK

PROCESS

Students own language

oral: report   written: journal
full-class   profile
small group   lists
paired   notes
interviews   drafts
surveys   forecasts
role plays   diagrams
tapes   propositions

PRODUCT

mode
form
register

PRESENTATION

feedback
analysis
evaluation
reflection

Language functions involved?
Teacher's language role?
Style of presentation?
What has been learnt by student?
What has been learnt by class?
What has been learnt by teacher?

wall displays are of the highest standard, frequently changed, imaginatively hung – perhaps this should be their responsibility. You may have displayed board games, or lists of questions, a graffiti board or unfinished work – writing in early draft form, the first paragraph of a narrative or expository piece – so that interplay between the display and the students can be encouraged and they are challenged by them to learn.

But you should also be looking for other audiences beyond the classroom. If you have been able to make cross-curricular links with other departments your students' research will have been deepened and their products made more presentable. The work might go to other classrooms, or the staffroom, or find a permanent home in the school or town library. It might form a display in the school foyer or in another school or a public place in the town. Perhaps it will get into the local media. It might be sent to the Architects Department in the Council House, to the newspaper office or the office of Animal Rights. If the outcome is a dramatic presentation you might take it round the upper school English classrooms, make an evening of drama for the parents or record it on videotape for a wider circulation.

Detailed advice intended to help your students achieve very high standards in this work is given in *Initiatives*. On Repromaster 5 of *On and Off the Record* appears advice on Designing a Popular Magazine, and Repromaster 36 carries a transcript of Fay Godwin talking about experimenting with photography. Repromaster 26 of *The Right Idea* deals with video camera technique and Repromaster 3 advises on the production of a tape and slide show. There is advice about making videos on Repromasters 11 and 12 of *Campaign,* and effective techniques for good quality audio recording are given on Repromasters 4, 10, 12 and 13 of *Opening Up the Airwaves*.

Presentation bestows purpose on the process; the nature of the presentation determines the nature of the process. By working for a given audience and interacting through the presentation with that audience, the producers and the members of that audience all gain.

National Curriculum for English

The material and assignments in the *Initiatives* books are entirely appropriate to the National Curriculum for English. All aspects of the National Curriculum are amply and challengingly covered, including the drama and media studies elements and much besides. There is nothing in the programmes of study and, therefore, by definition, nothing in the statements of attainment that is not integral to the *Initiatives* approach.

English does not fit neatly into a framework of attainment targets and statements of attainment. Progress in this subject is not achieved by slogging through graded exercises but by absorption in and reflection on a wide range of language experiences.

Initiatives is not a course. The activities within it do not get progressively harder. The students, though, as a consequence of their earlier work, will progressively bring more to these activities, with the result that their achievement will steadily reflect greater understanding of the issues and greater subtlety of expression. You cannot, then, usefully aim to demolish a particular statement of attainment with a particular activity. If you did, you would unnecessarily limit your students' scope for learning. Instead, you should ensure that your programme of study, in this case the *Initiatives* books, provides each student with language experiences that do cover all aspects of the attainment targets and can generate time and again statements of attainment appropriate to your individual students' developmental needs. You should ensure too that your recording system is simple and accurate enough to provide you with the information you need on the progress of each of your students.

Speaking and listening in *Initiatives* work is habitual. Students are encouraged to work in pairs, small groups and as a class on a wide range of activities. They are asked to discuss as themselves and in role, to interview, to conduct surveys, to negotiate, to take part in simulations. In short, they are expected to function orally in all the situations they are likely to encounter outside the school context. They are, what is more, required to function effectively in a range of small group roles, as visiting expert, as protagonist and as chairperson. They will be encouraged to present their finished work to different audiences and using a variety of techniques. And they will be encouraged to reflect on their work and the work of their classmates and to evaluate it.

Literature from the British Isles, Asia, Africa, the Far East, Europe and the Americas is represented in *Initiatives*, and among the pre-twentieth century British writers included are Shakespeare, Keats, Tennyson, Hardy, Austen and Mrs. Gaskell. As well as novels there are newspapers, magazines, short and minimalist (Bob Taylor) stories, poems, stories from the oral tradition (Julie Fullarton), examples of Old English (*Faeder Ure*), autobiography (Christopher Nolan), biographies (*People of Providence*), journals (*I Walked by Night*), legend (Dick Turpin), fairy story (*Tom Tit Tot*) and myth (Perseus). Throughout, students are encouraged to explore the craft of writing, to examine the writing for evidence of the writer's standpoint, and the text itself for 'features of presentation' which betray its deeper purpose. You will be working with demanding, sometimes little known, literature, looking at genre, form, narrative structure, the author's relationship with her reader, how effects have been achieved, how points of view are presented, helping your students in their 'quest for meaning' to become 'independent readers'.

The National Curriculum requires that students are enabled 'to develop more conscious and critical control over the writing process'. The *Initiatives* writers encourage students to achieve this by, in the first place, presenting a wide range of activities that have genuine purpose for the student. Within this context they pay particular attention to the processes of composition, with drafting being recognised as intrinsic to meaningful writing. There is plenty of opportunity for students to write in narrative, descriptive and expository modes and in a variety of forms. The emphasis throughout is on the precise expression of meaning and the need to meet the requirements of a specific readership.

From the subtitles of the four Resourcebooks
The Language of Life
The Language of Story
The Language of Reporting

The Language of Expression,
it is clear that *Initiatives* is based on a study of the
English language. By encouraging the students to use
their own language in a variety of specific contexts, the
writers of *Initiatives* believe students will learn more
about how the language works. But there is also
throughout the books an attempt to get the students to
stand back and analyse the language dispassionately. The
material the writers have marshalled, the use to which
they have put it and the approaches that you as the
teacher have been recommended to take, are all intended
to ensure that the students will develop a clear sense of
• the history of English;
• the structure of the language;
• the characteristics, lexical and grammatical, of different
dialects;
• changes in word use and meaning;
• attitudes society has to dialect;
• attitudes society has to language change;
• the persuasive power of language;
• the layers of meaning language has,
and that from these growing awarenesses the criteria for
independent judgement and taste can develop.

Your local authority might have provided you with a
system for recording your students' progress through the
statements of attainment, but in case it hasn't, pages 39
and 40 contain examples of a system based on the
following principles:
• It requires a descriptive approach. You do not tick a
statement of attainment when you are convinced it has
been achieved; you describe as briefly as possible what
your student did.
• You describe on this record not only achievements that
relate specifically to a statement of attainment but
anything that you regard as 'a significant language event'
for that student.
• You add the date beside your comment to indicate when
the event occurred.
• You sign your comment to indicate when a particular
statement of attainment has been achieved and the
student 'can do' it.
• The comments you make should be full enough to be of

use to you at a later date when you are discussing your students' progress with him, another teacher or his parents.

• You write comments about the Speaking and Listening attainment target on the day the 'event' occurs, and comments about Reading and Writing perhaps every half term.

• You should aim not to replicate work. Try to use the system in such a way that it can be used for recording progress over the years and for reporting formally to parents.

• You should decide how you can involve the student in the evaluation of his work and the subsequent recording process. It is a sound principle that he should be involved throughout, but you need to work out a routine that is genuinely collaborative and yet practical. Do you fill in the form together? Does he keep his own version? Does he have a duplicate copy? (What importance do you give to his perceptions?)

The system has these two further characteristics:

1. One sheet of A4 (both sides) contains the whole of one level – across the four attainment targets.

2. A plastic spine holds the record together.

These simple expedients have clear practical benefits. They allow you to

• withdraw a completed sheet for safe keeping in the main book or filing system.

• carry with you only the papers – covering two or three levels – that you need.

• include in the plastic spine any evidence or other material you currently need.

• manage the recording system with comparative ease.

ENGLISH LEVEL SIX

Name ....

Date (to be noted when strand completed)

1. Speaking and Listening

contribute considered opinions or clear statements of personal feeling to group discussions and show an understanding of the contribution of others.

use language to convey information and ideas effectively in a variety of situations where the subject is familiar to the pupils and the audience or other participants.

plan, organise and participate with fluency in a group presentation or performance.

show in discussion an awareness of grammatical differences between spoken Standard English and a non-standard variety.

2. Reading

read a range of fiction and poems, explaining in detail their preferences by talking and writing.

demonstrate, in talking and writing about literature, other texts and non-fiction that they are developing their own insights and can sustain them by reference to the text.

show in discussion that they can recognise whether subject matter in non-literary and media texts is presented as fact or opinion, identifying some of the ways in which the distinction can be made.

select from a range of reference materials, using appropriate methods to identify key points.

show in discussion of their reading an awareness that words can change in use and meaning over time and demonstrate some of the reasons why.

Name ....

Date (to be noted when strand completed)

Activity/Commentary/Signature

3. Writing

write in a variety of forms for a range of purposes, presenting subject matter differently to suit the needs of specified known audiences and demonstrating the ability to sustain the interest of the reader.

produce, independently, pieces of writing in which the subject matter is organised and set out clearly and appropriately and in which sentences and any direct speech are helpfully punctuated.

demonstrate the ability to use literary stylistic features and those which characterise an impersonal style, when appropriate, using Standard English (except in contexts where non-standard forms are needed for literary purposes).

recognise when planning that redrafting and revising are appropriate and act accordingly, either on paper or on a computer screen.

demonstrate through discussion and in writing grammatical differences between spoken and written English.

4 and 5. Presentation

recognise that words with related meanings may have related spellings, even though they sound different; recognise that the spelling of unstressed syllables can often be deduced from the spelling of a stressed syllable in a related word.

check final drafts of writing for misspelling.

write fluently and legibly.

show some ability to use any available presentational devices that are appropriate to the task, so that finished work is presented clearly and attractively.

ON AND OFF THE RECORD

As the title suggests, the main theme of this book is the sub-text: what is going on below the words or the pictures. *On and Off the Record* will help students become more aware of how they are made to respond in the way they do, more conscious that behind the scenes is the writer or photographer with her perspective or angle, her own personal baggage, the editor who will have her say, and society, too, with its own value systems. There will, therefore, be techniques of writing and editorial devices intended to effect a particular response in the reader. By working through the material assembled in this book in an investigative and reflective way the students will become more discerning and more independent as readers.

To help the students with the early work on photographs I would ask them to make themselves two cardboard L's to use as a moveable framing gadget. I would work with the full class up to page 13 on discussion and brainstorming as an introduction, then divide the students into groups of three or four for the magazine work, which I would encourage them to share on its completion.

If you have close contact with the Technology or Art department you might be able to work on some of this material in a cross-curricular way. For example, to enlarge whole photographs or sections of photographs would be useful, and to mount displays in a professional manner helpful to the students who produced the work and the rest of the class.

Unit 1
Page 16/17

The paired work on Putting it on the Record on Repromasters 1 and 2 could give rise to a full class discussion on the nature of reproting for different perspectives to be shared at the start.

You might set up a triangulation exercise in your class as another experiment in reporting. A student from your class and another teacher sit in on one of your classes and afterwards the three of you compare notes on precisely what happened, in terms of your style as a teacher and what was learnt.

You might also want your students to find a graffito in their locality for their homework and to write a poem as a commentary on it in the next session.

41

Page 20

The pairs of students working on the same article could get together after a time to compare notes and reach agreement on their interpretation. They could then plan an illustrated presentation for the rest of the class so that they could share their understanding.

Page 21

I would want to take the full class through the first section very carefully so that by the end everyone was at home with the numerous technical terms in the passage. The paired work on Repromaster 4 would be a means of reinforcing this new understanding by talking it out. How you group your class for the production of 'Your Future' will depend on how long you want the project to run. It is something that the whole class could do together, with each student taking a particular job, in which case the magazine could be produced in a week; or something that a group of four could do over a month. Again, close liaison with Art or Design might be of mutual benefit.

Page 24

Although there is a great deal of scope for students to determine the way the Mass Observation will be run, you need to have thought out the logistic issues carefully beforehand:
•Would the whole class work responsibly during class time?
•Could you get all the pairs in position in class time with enough time for any meaningful observation to take place?
•Could you extend a session that fell before or after lunchtime or last period in the afternoon?
•Where will you get the cameras and tape recorders from?
•How long do you want the observation itself to last?
•Will you hold it on what is in any case a special day, a festival or a sporting event?
•Will you do a dawn or dusk observation?
•How will you bring together all the material to make a coherent display or presentation?

Unit 2

You might want to prepare for this work by assembling in the classroom books about 'legendary' figures from the past and present, people like Annie Oakley, Emmeline Pankhurst, Sylvia Plath, La Passionaria, Pat Garrett and Billy the Kid, Bob Dylan and Mohammed Ali. You might make a collection of appropriate biographies, novels, history books and ballads. I think I would start with the tape of *Turpin Hero* and Repromasters 8a and 8b to establish the right feel for the unit. Students might write a piece on someone they admire greatly and swap this work with a classmate, who will look in detail at the kind of language that has been used.

Page 28

You will know whether your students need you to read these extracts to them as a class. Suggestions as to how you might like to group your students for the activities that follow are clearly given. You might like to ask a History colleague if she would be available to offer any help in the classroom for this work. Such collaboration could have positive repercussions in English, History and Geography National Curriculum work. People from different age groups or walks of life would probably have quite different sets of 'legendary' figures: it might be interesting to do a survey on this so that comparisons could be made.

You might also want to direct your students' attention to the language that is used in these accounts. Do they sound authentic? If so, what gives them this quality? Encourage the students to analyse the language clearly to find out what the tone of authenticity is due to.

One way of working with this material would be for your students to choose which of the three 'legends' they would like to study, and for the three groups that would then form to work independently. When the work had been completed each group could present its findings to the other two groups. In any event, you might want to encourage the students to reflect on how much they now really know about these figures, what the problems are in getting to know what famous people are really like and why it is we need to know what is the reality beneath the image.

Page 41

Although you may be disinclined to go through the whole class with these presentations because you feel students

43

will get bored once they have had their stint, I would recommend hearing from everyone. Students will be used, by now, to sharing work and ideas and giving feedback and, in any case, they are always interested in hearing about each other.

<table>
<tr><td>Page 42</td><td>The class might like to discuss why it is that we are often so keen to debunk a famous, even 'legendary' figure. They might be reminded of recent biographies of the pop legends – Elvis Presley, John Lennon and Bob Dylan.</td></tr>
</table>

Unit 3
Page 44/45

Research into the roles would make a very interesting homework assignment. The initial contract, with the person being considered for the interview and the pre-interview meeting, might be homework, too, but might be done by students during their English lesson if they are reliable. Because this is a comparatively tightly defined task it might be appropriate for students to whom you would like to give a first opportunity for out-of-classroom work. You will find this work extremely useful in developing your students' interviewing techniques, and to get as much benefit as you can in this respect I would let the period of reflection be long.

Page 47

There is further opportunity for out-of-school work here. It will be necessary for some students to consult reference books in the central library unless, with the school librarian's permission, they arrange for appropriate books to be sent into school. Other sources of information ought to be used too, though, so you will have to decide whether you are going to use homework time for this or allow several students to work in the town during English time. If you decide on the latter, make sure the purpose is clear and see the students for a quick debrief when they return. Try to ensure that the reports are presented attractively – you might want to enlist the help of another department – and, if your students wish to use visual aids, make sure they have had the opportunity to produce high quality material. They should decide on the appropriate audience.

Page 48

You might want to follow up this work with
• a look at some of W. H. Auden's poems of the same

period;
•a written response to the Brecht poems;
•a look at the September 1989 issue of *Books for Keeps*, which is on censorship with James Watson the main writer.

Page 50-52

You will probably want to read these to the class yourself and deal with the issues, as they are raised, in class discussion. The work here, on the techniques writers use to give their writing the ring of truth, is very important and might be substantiated further by a careful look at a short story by Luis Borges or H. G. Wells. You might like students who choose to write about the place they live 'from the point of view of a complete stranger' to do it in role as someone who
•is in mourning;
•is agoraphobic;
•is naturally optimistic;
•doesn't like modern architecture;
•always exaggerates; or
•is in love.

Page 55

When the students have decided in their small groups what the two missing children's rights should be, the class should come together to share these conclusions and decide which two have most support. All those chosen could go up on the graffiti board, and any others as they occur to students.

Page 56

The instructions for this major piece of work are very clear, but you will need to familiarise yourself with all the material – the information in the book, the tape recording and the repromasters – beforehand, and recognise the six distinct stages:
•The whole class studies the material, listens to the recording, discusses what might have happened.
•Groups of six are formed (five representatives plus one other) and students take on their roles, reading the appropriate repromaster.
•Meeting of interest groups to prepare their defence.
•The Committee of Public Inquiry meets – read Repromaster 27.

• Each group produces a report and circulates it.
• A period of reflection, on how much truth emerged, and by what means; a comparison of what happened in each group.

Unit 4
Page 62

I would try hard to get the right blend of students in each of the groups for this activity. Each member will have a demanding job, but those with less mastery of language will have to take on one within their capabilities. Because there is a lot of responsibility attached to each job and all the students will have to report back on the three stories as experts to their group, there is an opportunity for everyone to succeed, in their own eyes and those of their classmates.

Page 64

When discussing the titles of newspapers, I would like the students to agree to a title that they would give a present-day newspaper.
The journals of work in progress are an effective means of encouraging the student to reflect on his learning and to bring to consciousness his work practice. They are for his own benefit, and perhaps you would treat them as his own confidential property unless he makes it clear that he is happy to share them. He might want to keep them separate from his other journals or incorporate them: I would expect that decision to be up to him.

Page 67

I think you should ensure students do not work for too long with the same classmates in pairs or small groups, but recognise the value of working with a range of people. If there is a disinclination to form new partnerships continually a routine would have to be established.
The conclusion to this piece of work would be in three stages:
• the presentation;
• the explanation of why certain decisions were made;
• the class evaluation of the presentation.

Page 68/69

I would have the examples of hype, collected for a homework, written up on the graffiti board.
After the presentations and the class evaluations, students might like to do the exercise Making the Most of It on

Repromaster 32 and follow it with a piece of writing entitled
•Still waters run deep;
•Looking back on my moment of glory;
•Nobody else noticed.

Page 70/74

To ensure that the students give the newspaper reports on the Dikko case adequate attention I would read them all out to the students then ask them to read them through again. You might be able to get hold of copies of one or two of the original newspapers, which would provide an interesting backdrop to the work. I would expect this material to have quite an impact on the students, so would want to give them time to reflect on it and discuss it in some detail, in small groups and as a full class. The outcomes of their research, too, might be surprising to some, so I would provide the opportunity for those who continued to follow news stories with an analytical eye to bring up the subject again should they want to. I would also reinforce the point by giving a high profile to the Angles work on Repromasters 33a and 33b.

Page 75/76

Students will want to be able to explore the implications of Kate Adie's talk in group and class discussion. I would like them to think about how, if you are a reporter, you have to 'set your feelings aside'; and how 'one of the things you often do with reporting is not to put adjectives in'. Students might want to write a piece about a public matter that has upset them emotionally, dispassionately and without using adjectives.
And they might like to study Old Testament journalism as it appears in stories like David and Goliath, Moses in the Bullrushes or Crossing the Red Sea to see what techniques of reporting were used then; and to rework these or other stories for one or two of our contemporary newspapers.

Unit 5
Page 78/79

A homework in which students found what might have been a deliberately set-up photograph would give rise to a classroom display giving a context to this unit's work.

Page 81

I would have five groups of students for this, one for each option. I would ask them to present their work in the order it appears here and, using the class presentation almost as a rehearsal, would ask the students to arrange for a presentation to another class.

Page 85/86

You will probably want to ensure all the extracts are used by encouraging the groups to take one extract each. While the students are working on the text there will be a good opportunity for you to work alongside, helping them recognise how the writers have used the language. When the students report back to the class they will consolidate their understanding by finding their own words for it. I should make sure there are newspapers available so that the work can develop accordingly.

Page 87/88

I would make sure that the seven subjects are all covered, that the statements are carefully prepared and that the evaluation of presentations is thorough. The journalists' recording procedures should also be shared and the means (of style and content) by which the material has been condensed into a ninety-second slot examined by students in pairs.

Page 93

I think I would regard the news team work as a rehearsal for the more demanding local radio news; but I would have six students working on Repromaster 37 during these activities, carrying out a thorough investigation of their local newspaper. Remember that each radio news group swaps its 'possible news stories' with those from another group, so that each is working with unfamiliar material; and ensure that conditions for the making of pre-recorded tapes are as good as you can make them. Again, because the 'live shows' should be stimulating, especially if the rehearsals iron out all the creases, it would be a pity if the audience couldn't be beyond the immediate class.

Page 94/95

I would regard this as a very important piece of work. I'd want all three activities to be covered by one or other of the groups and would devote several weeks of class time and homework time to it. If the compilations were done thoroughly a great deal of worthwhile work would be generated, from making 'phone calls to fix up visits from

48

experts to visits in the evening to the sports club to interview the captain of a local team. The finished products should be published to a high standard and presented in a local public forum – the library, arts centre or club rooms – where they could be on display for a time. On the other hand, you might prefer this activity to be much more low-key, work done by students in spare moments over a long period of time. There are advantages to this approach, but it might be difficult to sustain students' interest.

Unit 6
Page 102/104

Some of your students might want to move from this work to look at the book of photographs and poems entitled *Remains of Elmet*, at the front of which Ted Hughes wrote "Fay Godwin set out to capture some impressions of this landscape at this moment, and her photographs moved me to write the accompanying poems" (see page 44/45 of *The Right Idea*). Your students could write their own poems to accompany their own photographs (or photographs of others) of where they live, or they could swap their pictures with those of a classmate and write poems to accompany them. The next stage would be to see how successfully words had reflected or extended the qualities of the pictures.
Ted Hughes has collaborated with artists in some of his other poetry books. He worked with the photographer Peter Keen in *River*, with Leonard Baskin in *Under the North Star* and *Flowers and Insects* and Reg Lloyd in *What is the Truth?* and *The Cat and the Cuckoo*. Some of your students might like to take one of these books and explore, in a group, the effect on the reader of such a collaboration, seeing how one medium works alongside another.

Page 105/107

I would introduce the Dallas interview by having two students role playing the interview in front of the class. Then the students would reread it to themselves. When your students are considering how well they communicated their 'unforgettable experience' they should focus their main attention on the tape, using the transcript to pinpoint what was said. They need to remember that they are in the oral mode, which is different in its nature from the written. They should try to be explicit as to how they might improve next time and, perhaps, spend time thinking why it is that sometimes oral communication seems to work better than at other times (and written communication, too, come to that). The second 'pointer for discussion' should be given plenty of time, and could lead to an analytic piece of writing. The sets of guidelines for conducting interviews should be compared, a consensus reached, the agreed set published and referred to and modified as experience dictates.

Page 108/109

You could take the full class through this with no written work. If students want to make their own magazine, though, I would have them working in groups, collaborating in pairs and as whole groups (four-six) with an 'editor' overseeing the work. Comparisons would be interesting, because the same place and the same format would generate very different magazines.

Page 110/111

It would be useful to the students on completion of this piece of work to be able to interview the editor of their local newspaper to get first hand an expert's point of view on these issues.
When your students are in groups discussing their poems (which you might want to read to the whole class first), ask them whether they find the accompanying illustrations in the book helpful. If they had been editing the book, what illustrations would they have used? What would they have been trying to do with the illustrations? They might want to write about
• a place associated with tragedy:
  – Hungerford (massacre)
  – Lockerbie (plane crash)
  – Balcombe Street (siege)
  – San Francisco Bay Area (earthquake)
• or mystery:
  – Ayres Rock
  – Wastwater
  – Tintagel
  – Bermuda Triangle
• or of fiction:
  – Lyonesse

– Transylvania
– Atlantis
– Shangri-la,

trying to capture a sense of the place itself and communicate something of the complex feelings that they have about it.

Page 114

If the place which a student wants to write about is not too distant he should have the opportunity to spend some time there before writing his poem. Perhaps time out of class, homework time or time during the weekend could be spent getting a deep feel of the place, absorbing the atmosphere and tuning his senses acutely into as many of the details as he can. He might want to use his journal to jot down phrases as they come to him.

Unit 7
Page 118/125

I think the intimacy of paired work is appropriate to the material and activities on *The Other Side of the Hedge*. It also suits the poacher/gamekeeper confrontation. It would be useful, though, for the full class to come together from time to time to compare notes and share anecdotes. From my own experience of memoirs – as oral reminiscences – the main weakness is the natural tendency to gross exaggeration! A poacher I knew was as good a storyteller as he was a shot, but he could certainly convey the 'feel' of the life style through his anecdotes. You might want to feed extracts from Barry Hines' fine book *The Gamekeeper* into discussions. Also the Sam Peckinpah film *Pat Garrett and Billy the Kid* would be intersting in this context, particularly if it were possible to see the two versions so that students could compare the more complete later edition with the much cut first one.

Page 126/135

This material represents the climax of the work on interviewing that has been a theme in this book. I'd play the tapes at least twice, reading the text alongside. I'd follow carefully the author's suggestions for grouping the students: the first work should all be done in pairs, then, on page 130, when the subject is documentary techniques, students should work in groups of four. Independent pieces of writing should follow, their titles negotiated between student and teacher. "Everybody in Some Way is

Interesting ... " should also be worked through by using tape and text concurrently: it is essential as a precursor to Sprowston.

For this major piece of work you will need to establish structure and focus by being very clear what you and your students' aims are. You will need to decide with the students which groups in the community will be interviewed: Tony Parker suggested the vicar, the police, pub landlords, elderly people, and so on. And you need to decide how you intend to use your information. Tony Parker's suggestions included a display of diaries, a scrapbook, a tape for the local library and an article for the local paper. Although students might work in groups of four to six, much of the work will be done in the community, during class time or after school, which suggests it would be more practical for students to pair up. Interviewing would be more satisfactory in pairs and homework could be collaborative. Throughout, students should remember Tony Parker's insight that all interviews are rivetting, and that they should concentrate on all aspects of the exchange, the content of the words, the style of the delivery, the questioning technique and its effect, the nature of the answers and the interaction between interviewer and interviewee. The belief needs to be there, too, that everyone is an expert, and that if this is not being revealed on any occasion, thought has to be given to the whole interviewing technique.

There may not be people with Tony Parker's experience in interviewing working for your local television or radio station but there will be professionals who could offer a great deal of helpful advice, even supervision. It might give your project more dynamism and coherence if you were able to link up with an expert in the field. And such a link might provide your students with the medium for presenting their material, which might make all the difference to their sense of purpose.

THE RIGHT IDEA

Unit 1
Page 7

After the students have brainstormed ideas, rank ordered them individually, then agreed to a final rank order and presented the list to the rest of the class, you might want them to reflect on what they have just done, to evaluate the usefulness of that process. Researching the working methods of writers will require deciding on a set of questions for the survey then thinking about how the questions should be posed. In fact your students will be able to interview some writers and artists in the school community and locally and this work can be done in lesson time and for homework. But they will also want to look for material in books, and their most profitable source will probably be those poetry and extract anthologies that contain introductions by the contributors. There will also be books written by writers and artists that you will need to make available in the school library and provide access to in the local library.

Page 9

I don't think I would have each student hot-seated in turn in front of the class. The interest would begin to ebb after a while. It might be more stimulating, once everyone in each group has performed, for the class to share insights gained from the group activities.

The gallery tours, on the other hand, might be shared with the whole class, and variety would be provided if one group were to take four paintings from different stages of the work of say, Goya, Cezanne, Kandinsky or Klee – all artists whose styles changed markedly in their careers. The class might be invited to discuss what it is about certain paintings that makes them so famous or popular: does popularity equate to quality?

Page 11

You might want to show the class various still-lifes to make the point that the painting reveals as much of the artist as it does the subject. Then, when the descriptions have been completed and are being shared, ask the writers what it was that they wished to convey and compare that to what the audience felt had been communicated. Did the words do what the writers had intended them to do?

Page 12

There is a good opportunity with these options for

53

students to work in the community during class time and/or for homework. For these options to be available to all students the school will require photographic equipment, and darkroom facilities would enable students to experiment with their work. There are many possibilities here. Some of your students might like to investigate the designs of great architects like Le Corbusier, Mies van der Rohe or Frank Lloyd Wright or modern developments like Welwyn Garden City, the King's Cross or the Chelsea Dock projects, or a new theme or industrial park. Others might want to trace the changes that have taken place over the last fifty years to their own town. Once the work is completed it should be shared with the whole class, which means the final product should be attractive and the presentation carefully prepared.

Page 13

This debate should reflect the formality of the council chamber. The advice for students on Repromaster 19 is useful. I would arrange the chairs in concentric semi-circles with the chairperson in the front centre. Students should think things through before the debate and make their contribution only when invited from the chair. You could use other issues for the debate, like whether churches should be knocked down to make way for car parks, whether Prince Charles should have his way over modern architecture or whether bungalows should be allowed. There might be a local issue – the sculptures in the forest in Cumbria or the replacement for the Rotunda Tower in Birmingham – that could be discussed instead.

Page 18

To emphasise the fact that our heads are full of stories crouched to leap out, give all the students a blank piece of paper and a verb in the past tense like 'was walking'. Ask them to start writing a story using this verb in the first sentence. After half an hour, see how they are getting on. Ask them to share their work. You will, of course, be able to share with the class twenty-five beginnings of stories, all different and all potentially interesting. You might want to feed in some of the thoughts in a book like John Fowles' *The Ebony Tower*, where the author explores the nature of story writing. You might want to hold a class

54

discussion on where all these ideas come from. Or where, indeed, the words themselves come from. Where do we store them? And why do they only sometimes come flowing out?

Page 19
You might also want to feed in poems on the creative act, like *The Thought-Fox* by Ted Hughes. Other revenge poems you might want to use are written by Dryden and Pope, and recently Simon Rae and Wendy Cope.

Page 20/21
Teachers have a bad image in poems. You will remember Miss Walls in *Death of a Naturalist* and Miss Creedle in Gareth Owen's poem *Miss Creedle Teaches Creative Writing*. The English teacher in Ian McEwen's *The Cement Garden* is a different sort of character, though his Headteacher makes things difficult for him. Ask your students exactly how they would like their English teachers to be. Ask them to compare *The Prime of Miss Jean Brodie* with *Dead Poets' Society*.
I would encourage students to send letters to writers. Often they will get a reply and this can be very encouraging. Ask the students why they think writers do write. Play them Van Morrison's celebratory song *Rave On, John Donne* and see what they make of that.

Page 22
I would have the students working in groups of eight with two taking each question and sharing conclusions. The fourth option might be made more meaningful if you were able to persuade a small panel of teachers from other disciplines to come to your classroom temporarily to help provide information.

Page 23
Your students might look at the creative energy of Picasso, or Barnes Wallis or Clive Sinclair, or the artistic skills and influence of Heath Robinson as illustrator of *The Rubáiyát of Omar Khayyám* or Keating or Foreman.
They might want to design a building to go into a prime site in their town and present it to the class with all the supportive arguments, or decide what should be built alongside the National Gallery in Trafalgar Square.

Page 24/25
Your students might want to keep a journal, in which to

jot down ideas or phrases as they occur to them, for later reference.

They might want the opportunity to look thoroughly at this subject for a long time before writing. I have heard Leslie Norris say that he was once taken by Ted Hughes to look at his bull. What Leslie assumed would be a fifteen minute visit took all day, with the poet laureate absorbed in the spectacle of his animal. It is concentration like this that enables Ted Hughes to create such minute detail and revealing imagery.

Page 27

A focus on the writing process is extremely important, and you should try to get students to recognise precisely how they do write so that they can compare practice and try out a range of methods to find which suits them best.

Unit 2
Page 30/31

Your students would produce more convincing self-portraits if their penfriends were real. You might wish, therefore, to twin with another school in the borough or elsewhere in the country so that frequent exchange of letters is possible. Other ideas you might like to use are:
•Look at yourself as an old person, your old hands, legs, wrinkled face, and reminisce about the years that have passed.
•Look at your friend after the passage of fifty years and reminisce about the youth you spent together.
•Allow your past to flash through your mind as people say it does when drowning.
•Describe yourself as if you are Van Gogh or Francis Bacon or Lucian Freud, putting portraits separated by twenty-five years side by side.
•Describe yourself from the psychiatrist's couch, in stream-of-consciousness.
For this you will need to do plenty of paired work so that students can probe their memories deeply. It will need to be handled with delicacy.

Page 32/33

Most students will have a member of their family who is keen on family history; one or two will have the beginnings of a family tree already. But you will need to show them what family trees can look like by providing one of your own or finding one from the start of a family

56

novel or history book.

There are interesting homework assignments in this section, and possibilities for very varied and imaginative work. Writing could be comic – lost rings, no organist, an offensive speech from the best man – or emotional – meetings after many years, divorced father's presence, tears from mother. Work could lead into a study of *The Rime of the Ancient Mariner*. All this work should be well-presented, shared and evaluated by the rest of the class.

Page 35

You might like to feed into the options poems like Carl Sandburg's *In a Break* and Richard Eberhart's *The Groundhog* which slip from surface life to darker issues. Your students could begin with a description of a mundane experience and allow their thoughts to drift to something philosophical and profound. The third option should produce extremely interesting work which would make an informative display, especially if the pieces by the same author were presented orally by him and displayed side by side with the expressive piece.

Page 36/37

Some people find they write best when sitting in a special place. You might suggest that your students for homework think about where they would be most comfortable and stimulated to do this written work.

Page 38

To bring relations into school for discussions about the old days should be encouraged: it strengthens links between school and community, with families and across generations, and it offers scope for the study of language in real circumstances.

Page 40/41

You will have the practical difficulty here of an insufficient number of tape recorders. Offer the taping work as an option to those students you can provide machines for, and ensure that next time there is work of this sort, other students will have the opportunity to do it. By organising things so that each group of students does its recording on a particular evening and machines are handed over to the next group the following day, you could involve a good proportion of the class. For students to get the best results they will need to think carefully about the right conditions for interviewing: read *On and Off the Record*, page 46. You might also read the Betty Rosen book on oral storytelling *And None of it was Nonsense*.

Do you want your students to transcribe their stories? If so, should they try to reproduce the dialect? Do you want them to discuss the nature of the stories they collect, their content, messages, attitudes to gender; the quality of the storytelling, the techniques of the storyteller, what the story has lost in transcription? Should they write up the story in standard English and compare the oral and written forms?

The finished autobiographical pieces could be put together to make a 'Book of the Class'.

Page 43

Students could plan their approaches to the role play situation sitting in their interest groups. Once the preparation is complete the student in the chair could invite the first contribution and the exchange of arguments, formally directed, could begin. A debate like this might begin with only the spokesperson of each group speaking, but this conversation could, after the initial exchange, be broadened to allow anyone to have his say.

Page 46

Your students' Martian poems might be views from an unusual angle – 'Under poems', for example: poems from under the sea, under the table, car, bed or stairs; in a mine or in a wrestling match – or from a particular perspective, such as from a driver's point of view: a taxi, bus, train, lorry, barge or bike driver, or a balloonist. They might want to make anthologies, in groups, of poems from different planets, on famous buildings, statues or paintings, of job songs, or the stories of a group of people on the way to a match or a festival.

Page 47

If you are able to get large reproductions of any of these paintings, or other paintings that would be similarly provocative, it might be advantageous to your students.

Unit 3
Page 50/51

I think I would want to have a backcloth of advertisements on the classroom walls for this unit of

58

work, and would ask my students to find one or two particularly interesting ones which we would then put together for a display. It might still be possible to find old metal advertisements and many students will be able to call on the services of relations inclined to hoard who would be able to give or loan bygone materials. To continue the 'real' theme, I would encourage students to promote a band or singer from the school because there would be an immediacy to this and the possibility of interviews, photographs and so on. I would also try to involve the Technology department whenever possible.

Page 52/53

In the role play you might want students to take on particular tasks – to write the slogan, to compose the jingle and so on. Other situations might be the telephone promotion – "Hello, this is Barbara from ... ", the doorstep interview or the timeshare hassle on the pavement of Marbella or after the lavish hotel dinner.

Page 54/55

I should start the session in lively fashion by having as many students as seems appropriate selling their object in one minute. The 'barking' improvisations should be limited to one or two pairs of students, I should think, or the row would be unbearable – and unproductive. You really need a sound-proofed small room for an activity like that. If a pair of your students were able to persuade a market barker to be taped in full flow some very useful analysis of her 'patter' could be carried out using a transcription alongside the recording.

Page 56/57

I would link some of this work to the work in Unit 5 of *On and Off the Record*. Students in pairs could work carefully on an analysis of newspaper text. It might be necessary for them to feed their conclusions into a full class session for cross-fertilisation of ideas.

Page 58/59

This is a major piece of work that you will need to prepare for carefully. Unit 6 of *On and Off the Record* will be helpful. Enlist the Technology department to make sure the finished products are of high quality, and encourage your students to take surveys among the readers of the magazines to see how they might improve a second edition.

Page 60/61

Before your students draw up their *Which?* text you might want to give the activity more validity by inviting a statistician – from the Maths or Science department – into the classroom to answer questions. A survey or students' views of the product under scrutiny might provide useful data but the questions would have to be carefully prepared.

Page 62/63

I would take the whole class through these two extracts, and ensure that only the most able students attempted the very demanding third option. Your students might have an issue they would rather debate than those proposed here. Before preparations begin they should thoroughly discuss Repromaster 19, and they might like to study a recording of parliament in session or one of the speeches made by Martin Luther King or Neil Kinnock and think about rhetorical devices. A group of students might wish to do the work in *Campaign* or *Agony Column* at this point. If speeches on important issues were given frequently in school assemblies by students, the deliverers of these speeches and the audience would benefit greatly.

Page 64/65

I would organise the students into pairs for this activity, and offer these other suggestions for letter-writing:
•from one historical character to another;
•from a stiff-upper-lip public figure in trouble to his family, and back;
•to convey a story – see *Several Stories High*, Unit 6.
They might also wish to
•analyse the nature of letters read out on Radio 4 at 5.30 each evening: week's postbag would provide an interesting sample;
•read and review letters written by a famous writer, like John Keats or Sylvia Plath;
•in the role of a famous Victorian archaeologist – Carter or Schliemann – or an eminent explorer, write letters home to the family and to the profession giving news of a major discovery.
Repromaster 21 gives an example of a formal letter layout.

Unit 4
Page 68/69

Other poets who use newspaper stories as their inspiration are Adrian Mitchell, Bob Dylan and Simon

Rae. Your students might like to write a poem based on this article, or on another article they have recently read.

Page 70/71   See Unit 5 of **On and Off the Record** for ideas about a scrapbook.

Page 72/73   I would be very inclined to present this section as a whole series of options to be tackled briskly and light-heartedly then shared with the rest of the class.

Page 74/75   Play the tape to the whole class; then, with the students working in small groups, encourage thoughtful exchange of ideas prompted by what they have heard. It is important with the next activities that they remember how complex characters are. You might want them to look at the scene from *Oliver Twist* (page 85/86) at this stage, or one or two character descriptions from *Bleak House*.
I would have a small group present *The Real Inspector Hound* extract, after preparation, to the full class. And you might want to invite students to develop parody hero figures from science fiction, detective, romance or western genre; or to rewrite a famous short poem as a punk or a hippy or a yuppie might.

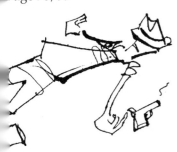

Page 76/77   John Branfield's book of short stories *The Day I Shot My Dad* has some pertinent things to say about writing. And *Books for Keeps* and *Signals* frequently have articles by writers on the business of composition.
I would have a small group prepare the play extract beforehand, either during class time or for homework, so that it could be performed to the full class at the appropriate time and to a good standard.
I would want my students to think carefully about the dialogue of the Pinter play and their own work: how realistic is it? Is it really how people speak? If it isn't, what are the differences? Why are there all those pauses in the Pinter? Are they realistic? Is realistic the same as naturalistic? Perhaps they should make a habit of writing down odd snatches of conversation in their journals.

Page 78/81   I would be inclined to have the class working in three groups at this point, one on the film script, one on the radio script and a third on *The Blackburn Files*. If the school does not have the equipment necessary for the first activity you could almost certainly borrow it from the Teachers' Centre. Although it is the preparation of the script that you want the students to concentrate on, it would give purpose if this work led to actual filming. For the radio script, if *The Listeners* does prove problematic, a narrative poem like *Conversation Piece* by Robert Graves or *By St. Thomas Water* by Charles Causley might fit the bill; and for the third activity a script by Willy Russell would be an interesting focus for study on realistic dialogue. If you wanted the groups to be smaller, two could work on the same or a similar activity. When a group has finished and has a product worth sharing with the full class a presentation should be made followed by an evaluation. Particularly good work should be given a wider audience, not necessarily from within the school.

Page 82/83

If you can't play an instrument perhaps one of your students can. If not, there will be someone in the school who will be able to provide accompaniment for those students who could be persuaded to sing their songs. For those who won't perform, the musician might be prevailed upon to sing as well. It is crucial that poems intended as lyrics are presented properly, as songs. You might supplement this performance by playing recordings of other work songs by blues singers, country and western singers and folk artists like Woody Guthrie and Pete Seeger. If you can get the words to go with the songs so much the better, then the students will be able to look at the lyrics in detail to analyse their characteristics and weigh their strengths.

Page 84/85

Dickens was a very melodramatic reader of his work by present-day standards. You will probably wish to read this extract out to the class and might want to emulate the author's style of delivery. To make an adequate comparison between the prose and the playscript you will want a small group, having prepared properly, to act out the scene in front of the class. If students do not feel that the play works particularly well they might like to make their own adaptation to see if they can improve on it.

I would present all this material together and ask students to choose which of the retelling options they would like to do. When the work has been completed, presented to the class and displayed long enough for all the students to have had a good look at the transformations there should be opportunities for reflection time. Would any of these artists have done better to have expressed this story or their vision in a different mode? Were any of them using a mode inappropriate to their theme? Have any of the students actually succeeded in transmitting the theme of one of the artists in a different mode? Have any partially succeeded? What have any of the students brought to the theme in their particular composition? What have they been able to express of themselves? Do they believe the comment that you can't make a great film out of a great novel? Why might there be some truth in this?

Unit 5
Page 94/98

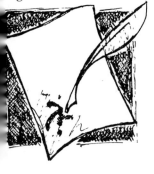

Students might like to read Brian Patten's *A Definition of Poetry* poem to see what he thinks poetry is and to write their own versions. I would want to take the students through these poems, reading them aloud then asking groups to take one of the poems and prepare a presentation on it for the rest of the class. Their presentations might take the form of dramatised reading, illustrated talk, dramatisation or explication using, say, an OHP.

You might want to use *Occurrence at Owl Creek Bridge* or the poem *Lost Love* by Robert Graves to illustrate heightened sense activity.

I would present Reading Poems in Groups and Reading a Poem on your Own as two separate lists of options, ask students in groups of two or three to select one activity from the first list and perform their completed works in front of the class. I would have students in pairs working on the activity of their choice from the second list and make a display of this work so that it could be shared.

Page 99/100

For this activity I would have one group of students working on a poem from the given newspaper article, a second from a newspaper or magazine article of their choice, a third from a list of titles from a poetry anthology, a fourth from advertising copy, a fifth using graffiti noted in the locality and a sixth using headlines found in the national press. When these had been completed, presented and displayed I would ask the students in the same groups to list whatever qualities they felt 'found' poetry like this might have, and to share these lists with the rest of the class.

Page 101/104

I would give my students examples of other sonnets and villanelles before asking them to try to devise a set of rules for either or try to write their own. I would also show them James Fenton's poem *Nothing* which has a clear but simpler form. I would invite anyone to try and write a poem using one of these forms, but it is an extremely difficult thing to do so I would offer alternatives too: perhaps some students would like, instead, to write a definition poem, like
• 'Love is ... ';
• 'What I like about ... ';
• 'I have a dream that one day ... '; or
• a poem listing thirteen ways of looking at – a cat or a cabbage or a king.

Page 105

I would give the class a sense of form by making an overhead projector transparency of a poem with a distinctive form and, revealing one line at a time, ask the class to predict how the poem will continue. They will focus particularly on content, but gradually the form will reveal itself too. On the same tack, you could prepare a poem using Bob Moy's computer programme, *Tray*, which a small group could work with, bringing the poem gradually to light as increasingly informed predictions reveal it.

Page 106/107

There are two main options here, the improvisation and the research work. You could add other options like inviting students to write their own ballads or to research into the work of modern folk/pop balladeers like Bob Dylan, Bruce Springsteen or Tracy Chapman: with these writers it would be the skills of condensing narrative, finding the striking image and capturing tension and drama that should be looked for. If each group is engaged in a different activity the whole class can gain a lot from the sharing process.

Page 108/109   You will need to be very supportive during this work, which might appear to the students at the outset to be easy but is actually extremely difficult.

An English Adviser, Andrew Stibbs, has written a series of Slug poems, parodies of famous poems in which he replaces the original subject with the slug. So he writes 'A slug came to my waterhole ... ' for D. H. Lawrence's *Snake* and Ted Hughes' poem becomes *Slug Resting* (for *Hawk Roosting*). Your students might like to try their hand at this sort of thing – Edward Pygge has also written a parody of *Hawk Roosting* called *Crow Resting* – but to do it successfully you need to know the work of the poet in question extremely well. Again, all students might be given the chance to try but they should not be given any illusions that it is an easy thing to do.

After this work on style and form your students should be encouraged to write about what they particularly want to find expression for, to work on their own but with a classmate to help with redrafting, and to recognise the difficulties and the rewards of finding (approximately) the words to reflect their thoughts and feelings.

Unit 6
Page 112   Students might like to review this list of questions from time to time, in case other important issues might be usefully included. A routine for honest criticism like the one outlined here should be habitual for the students in the form of self-evaluation, paired discussion or class reflection.

Page 113   Another activity would be for volunteers, after a period of preparation, to be hot-seated in front of the class and to defend their favourite television programme from arguments other students level at it. This could develop into paired work of a similar confrontational sort and then a written defence or review of the programme.

Page 116/117   The above work could be a precursor to this. I would be inclined to organise students into groups of five or six.

Page 120/121   You might want to link this material to Unit 6 of *On and*

Off the Record, or invite a group of students to begin work in the other book.

Page 122/123

Be sure that wherever possible your students relate this work to an actual placement and that when they discuss skills and qualities they have in mind a particular job. If the school has a record of achievement your student will be able to write this work in fair copy into this document. It will also be useful in thinking about future careers for students to analyse what skills and personal qualities particular jobs require and to consider the nature of their own.

Page 124/127

I would want students in groups of four each to work with the beginning of a novel from the point of view of giving advice to the author. You will want to choose your own novels, but I would certainly use the starts of *The Westing Game* by Raskin and *Treasure Island* by R. L. Stevenson. The advice would be written up and shared with the rest of the class.

There are various letters of complaint to be written in the last section. I would use the opportunity to experiment with different registers and tones, asking students to choose a specific level of formality and rudeness, so that some were frostily polite, some almost apologetic in their complaining and some plain angry. When the letters were shared, students could decide which style they felt would be most effective, which phrases most telling and how best to control and express a sense of grievance.

I would finish this unit by asking the students in groups of four to answer the following questions:
• Why do you talk the way you do?
• Why do you read the books you do?
• Do you listen to the words of the songs you like?
and to write a structured five hundred word essay on "Cos I like it!" and another on "Cos it's boring!", explaining clearly the reasoning behind the statements.

ROOTS AND ROUTES

Unit 1

There is a great sense of the fun to be found in language running through this book so I would bring this out whenever possible, trying to encourage in the students a pleasure in the sounds, connotations and resonances of words and an interest in exploring general, local or idiosyncratic features.

After the first taped discussion on students' experience of language in the classroom the opportunity is ideal for an open, free-wheeling class exchange of views on the same questions.

The third option might be structured to involve the whole class. The work could be divided into Talking (and Listening), Reading and Writing, and also delegated so that pairs of students could focus on particular classes.

Page 7

You will need to have a selection of good etymological dictionaries of first and surnames and place names to hand, perhaps collected from the central library, as a back-up resource for these activities. Your school librarian, too, might be able to support you with additional material.

I would want to offer further options here, like:

•Explore the nature of pets' names. What do they tell you about the relationship the pets' owners have with their pets?

•Explore the habit some people have of giving others a special nickname, looking at the sort of names used, and the reasons behind the habit.

•Collect a number of place names from two or three areas of the country (Yorkshire, Leicestershire, Dorset, Cornwall etc.) and compare them.

•Collect a number of place names from your area and analyse them. Then write to a student (through the Head of English) at a school in another part of the country for a list from his area, for comparison. What do you learn?

•Make a collection of first names given by pop stars or media personalities to their children – do they have anything in common?

•Analyse the history of the names of your school teachers, or the Cabinet and Shadow Cabinet of the present government, or English, Scottish, Welsh or Irish sports teams.

•Find a poem like the one on the next page which relies

largely for its effect on names. Look carefully at the names and the effect of the names. Then write your own poems set in an area you know well, making use of local names.

Dorset

Rime Intrinsica, Fontmell Magna, Sturminster
    Newton and Mebury Bubb
Whist upon whist upon whist upon whist drive
    in Institute, Legion and Social Club.
Horney hands that hold the aces which this morning
    held the plough
While Tranter Reuben, T. S. Eliot, H. G. Wells and Edith
Sitwell lie in Mellstock Churchyard now.

Lord's Day bells from Binghams Melcombe, Iwerne
    Minster, Shroton, Plush,
Down the grass between the beeches, mellow in the
    evening hush.
Gloved the hands that hold the hymnbook, which
    this morning milked the cow.
While Tranter Reuben, Mary Borden, Brian Howard
    and Harold Acton lie in Mellstock Churchyard now.

Light's abode, celestial salem! Lamps of evening
    smelling strong
Gleaming on the pitch pine waiting almost
    empty evensong;
From the aisles each window smiles on grave and
    grass and yew tree bough,
While Tranter Reuben, Gordon Selfridge, Edna Best
    and Thomas Hardy lie in Mellstock Churchyard now.
John Betjeman

Page 10

You might want your students to examine the language events they have recorded on Repromasters 2 and 3, to see which seems to have been particularly challenging or enjoyable or educative ...
I should run this set of options alongside the next, to avoid problems with tape recorders – it is likely that only one recording can be made at a time. When your students are comparing the spoken and the written versions I'd

encourage them to think fairly specifically about differences in words, phrases, constructions and in generalities of rhythm and explicitness.

Page 12

There are some helpful overlaps between the material here and at the end of *Several Stories High* that you might like to use. How successful this will be for each of your students will depend to some extent on serendipity but you will be able to help considerably by feeding in your own family history, as suggested, and bringing in your own materials, perhaps an heirloom that has passed through generations, perhaps photographs that show a family chair in a variety of settings over the years. I recently came across a book in which a Victorian ancestor of mine had collected poems, written by contemporary but now forgotten poets and by himself – that might create interest in the classroom and give an idea of what might be found in the attic at home. The presentation of this work should be taken very seriously and a launch, in the library perhaps, to an invited or open audience might be appropriate.

Page 14/17

I would use these activities at the beginning of English sessions to get things off to a lively, language-focused start. I'd cover the classroom walls with material that was generated from them, using the graffiti board in this instance for the 'new words for homework' etc. A total display like this would create an immersion in the language, making an excellent context for language use and study. Guides from the class could take visiting groups of students from other classes around the display, and you could help them with the special language skills such a role would require.

Page 18

I would ask the students out of role at the end of this activity to discuss the five main points again to determine how valid they themselves think they are.

Unit 2
Page 22/23

You will need to look carefully at the options in this book to see how it is best to group the students. For example, for the options on this page you might decide (in turn) on pairs, fours, pairs, pairs, fours, and use the final option as a long-running homework for some or all of the students to be doing over a period of time. Some students might want to take some of their research further and explore in detail the kind of words babies first learn and what combinations of words they make; and they might want to research into language phenomena like the secret language of some twins or the story of the wolf boy.

Of the options here you might want to use the written responses of parents for a wall display and the first words and phrases your students collect for the graffiti board. Early variations on words – paperment (pavement) and goosecumber (cucumber) – could be similarly collected, displayed and discussed.

I would find Repromasters 9, 10, 11 and 12 and their corresponding tapes particularly useful with small groups of students.

Page 27

The final option on this page might be done by a group of students very thoroughly. They might work closely with a class of children from a feeder primary school in an attempt to write books that are limited to the 250 most common words, but are also interesting and 'natural' to read. A project like this could also give rise to letter writing and telephone calls.

Page 32/33

I would be interested in exploring with the whole class where the words that Christopher Nolan uses in his writing came from. Where <u>did</u> he get them from? I would also want the students writing 'his' letter to use the language they feel he would have used.

I would want students, too, to consider what exactly they are up to when they are not fully listening; whether to be only half-listening is good enough; what full and active listening actually involves, and when fully listening, what they listen to and watch for. I would introduce Repromasters 18, 37 and 38 at this point.

Page 34/35

Seeing Voices, by Oliver Sacks, is an extremely readable book on sign language that I would try to make available in the classroom, alongside *Deafness: A Personal Account* by David Wright, which describes the importance of 'overhearing' as distinct from 'hearing'.

Page 40/41

You might want to ask the students one or two more questions about body language, like what they think hands clasped behind the head of a speaker conveys and what a speaker is doing by playing in various ways with her glasses; whether they think these gestures always mean the same and whether some – looking someone straight in the eyes during conversation, for example – can be misinterpreted. A group might like to look at a book on public speaking to see what can be made of criteria for judging a competition.

Page 43

A group of students might be interested in taking up the Animal Aid theme by doing the work in the Investigations Unit *Agony Column*. Before writing the letter students should consider very carefully why they believe an endangered species should be saved. They should also decide what is going to happen to their letters and write them bearing the intended audience in mind. In any case, a large display of letters should be mounted, perhaps in a public place such as a local doctor's waiting room, where there would be a large community readership. A display in such a place would require careful planning in and out of school and the proper procedure of gaining the Headteacher's approval at the outset would have to be followed.

In this context, students might be interested in discussing whether they think we are trapped by the kind of language we have developed into being a certain kind of animal. Would a different sort of language have given us different attitudes or beliefs or priorities?

Page 44/45

This could be developed into a major project involving the whole class for some time. It could involve several homeworks and one or two groups of students doing fieldwork in the community while the rest of the class worked with materials in the classroom.

Before the fieldwork was actually begun there would have to be considerable negotiation and planning to make specific focuses for the work. People from the community could be invited into the classroom for discussion. The resulting work might well be suitable for the local newspaper.

Unit 3

It ought to be re-emphasised that you need to have a good stock of text books about the English language to hand in your classroom, books on dialect, slang, quotations, history of the language, nature of the language, printing, publishing, as well as etymological dictionaries.

Page 54/55

I would want to take the whole class through this page slowly, with us all talking through the phrases that have become part of English. I'd want to issue copies of *Hamlet* and ask students in pairs to search for phrases that Shakespeare might have invented and are still current, and look at some passages from the King James version of the Bible for neologisms there. We would then try to decide, perhaps with the help of one or two student researchers, why the language seemed to be so particularly rich at that period of history. Students developing an interest in this area might wish to work in a group on some Chaucer or Langland, on *Gawaine* or *Philip Sparrow*.

For the modern section of the 'Child's Guide' it is likely there will be students in the class who would be able to help identify words that have only recently entered English. History and Geography teachers might be invited to take part in this work, and the Art department might be enlisted to help with the publication of the final document.

Page 56/57

I would want to talk the class through these pages, too. I'd want all the options on this page to be taken up and involve lengthy research. You might have two groups on each option, working separately but making sure they were not covering exactly the same material.

You might want to focus students' attention a little longer on spelling at this point:

• how important is spelling correctly?
• who is it important to?
• how can you learn to spell better?
• what common letter patterns <u>are</u> there in English?

Page 59

There are many opportunities in this book for your students to work closely on real activities with younger students in your own school or a feeder primary.

Advantage should be taken of these opportunities to build more understanding across the phases in such areas as approaches to English teaching, moderation and monitoring procedures. Options on 'selling a punctuation mark' and producing 'a handbook of punctuation tips' would require a great deal of research among the younger students, a lot of real talking and trialling, before a satisfactory result could be expected. A visit to a local primary school would not be hard to organise, particularly if it were only a small group of your students who were involved. It would almost certainly be a school close to your own and frequent visits would establish a working relationship.

Page 60

Groups of students might like to do research into who are the worst offenders when it comes to using jargon, making a list of questions on the subject that they would try to answer. Why, for example, do people use jargon? Is it ever necessary?

Page 63

Other activities you might like your students to choose from are:
•Look for occasions when Shakespeare or Ted Hughes uses a noun as a verb. Why does he do it? What is the effect?
•Rewrite a favourite story in 250 words and in 25 words. What is the difference between these two versions, in the stories and in the use of language?
•Imagine you are unable to communicate orally with other human beings and have a very important message to convey. Write your message in
– 100 words for a time capsule;
– 50 words for a message in a bottle;
– 25 words as a telegram;
– 10 words on a pigeon's leg.
What happens to the message and the language you use as the number of words gets smaller?

Page 66

I would want the class to discuss why the Lost Words on Repromaster 26 have dropped out of contemporary English.

Page 67

These options should all be presented to the full class on their completion. You might want to add some of your own, like:

• Explore John Lennon's song lyrics to see if he shows any sign of 'playing with language' in them. If he does, how effective is it?

• Analyse one of The Two Ronnies 'language' sketches to see exactly what they are doing.

• What features of English does Dave Allen find particularly amusing? Do you agree with him?

The option of producing a questionnaire is another opportunity for making links with the local primary school.

Unit 4
Page 72

You will probably still have a collection of books that were given to you as a child, some of which you could bring into the classroom to talk about and make a display which could be enhanced by books borrowed from other teachers. You might bring into the classroom a range of books borrowed from a feeder primary school or a major publisher of preselected collections of books for particular reading age levels. Such collections could be worked through carefully by a group of students who might

• find their own favourites, giving reasons;

• devise a list of criteria: what a book for children should have;

• decide on the qualities that the best books for children have;

• decide whether these qualities have been the same for more than one generation.

Some of this research might be done in a primary school with primary children. You would probably want the book writing to involve 'phone calls, letters and visits to the local primary school for discussions, responses and interviews before and after this option.

Page 74/75

You may want to link this letter writing work with *Several Stories High* (page 128/129) and bring into the classroom actual examples of material sent home by the school. Report comments which do not mean quite what they seem to say could be collected on the graffiti board. You might also be able to find examples of letters sent home from school to parents in literature, that would give a historical dimension to the work.

Page 76/77

Before doing the 'family talk' research you might want your students to prepare a sheet with the questions they intend to ask spaced out on it. The homeworks necessary to do justice to this option should be spread over some time and the consequence of the work could be role play acitvities that incorporate 'real' language use. You might want to include some simulations, too, showing, for example, a hitch-hiker being given lifts by a doctor, a beekeeper, a young man on the dole, a teacher and a member of parliament – or your own list that might serve your purpose better – with the class listening attentively and noting anything of interest in the passenger's use of language.

Page 80

The resulting reviews could be shared by students working in pairs or larger groups. This would enable writers to see in what ways they have satisfied the requirements of someone reading a review – have they given information of the right kind; have they given sufficient information; have they been personal enough; have the techniques of writing they have used been informative enough?

Page 81

I would include here for similar treatment *Duet*, a poem on a playground romance, written by Trevor Millum.

Page 82/83

I think I would take the whole class through this work so that responses could be shared throughout. Then I would ask students to choose from the options in pairs, so that the drafting process could be helped by their being with a classmate doing the same work.

Page 84/85

I would take the whole class through this work, too, pausing for as long as was necessary while the students reacted to the Plain English Society's fourteen rules. I would also want them to analyse material from some of the newspapers mentioned to see exactly what is being communicated by papers with very low or very high scores: what are the consequences of using very simple language to deal with complex thoughts and feelings? Perhaps you would like the students in small groups to conclude this section by discussing their favourite writers and the kind of language that they use. Students could each bring a page from a book by their favourite author for close analysis.

Unit 5
Page 90/91

I would take the class through this work, pausing for discussion when it seemed appropriate. Then I would offer all the options from both lists, including the investigation into community attitudes to dialect. A small group could carry out that study in school time if the students involved were responsible enough, for homework if not, and there would be a reporting-back session involving all the students to pull everything together. If there were local people with particularly interesting or outspoken views on dialect it might be worthwhile to invite them into the school at this point so that they could be interviewed in front of the class by carefully prepared students.

Page 93

A lot of fun could be had with the *Galed-ear-lawks* story. I'd have some pairs of students preparing a reading while others tried to rewrite *Goldilocks* in their own accent. We would then share the various interpretations.

Page 94/95

Again I would take the whole class through a reading of McCrum's article and follow it by asking groups to choose a riverboat, goldrush, cowboy, railroad, jazz, breakdancer or Silicon Valley scene for an improvisation incorporating the appropriate slang. After these had been performed, I would take the students through the rest of this work and ask them to choose from all the options.

Page 97

Conducting a community survey need not involve the whole class working out of the classroom. Much of the activity could take place in the classroom itself. I would have no more than two groups of students out of school at any one time. I'd make sure they were fully prepared before they went, knowing exactly what they were going to do, and I would validate the survey by limiting it to either

- one particular street or area;
- two contrasting streets or areas;
- a focal point – a street market, or parade of shops, or a queue;
- people all of the same profession or all working in the same place.

You might have favourite poems written in dialect you would like a group of students to respond to in writing. I would use *Ma Faddon* by Heather Harrison, and ask students to write a poem in their dialect about a local character.

Ma Faddon

Aad Ma Faddon sellt fish.
'N' ye knaa how owners grow te luk
just leyk their dogs?
Whey aad Ma Faddon grew te luk
just leyk a waalkin' cod.
Geet goggly eyes gawped oot from under 'er damp snood,
a wedgy sort o' fyess, blunt-nebbed,
'n' a doon-torned droopy gob.
she wore a white starched coat ower 'er slippy back o'
scales.
Nee laughs across thon marble slab.
Ower caad ye see.
She'd clamp 'er fingers roond a fistful o' sprats,
slap flat the spotty plaice,
'n' howk the gyuts oot iv a haddick
with a pile drivin' thumb.
She poked wet shillin's in yer hand for change
wi' five icicles for fingers, brittle leyk a claa.
'er money made yer dry hand smell.

"Haway, hinny, what ye want? Be sharp!"

Ma Faddon nivvor had the teym te wait,
ne teym te lissen. And as ye knaa
ne cod ivvor smiled.

Now the green shop's gyen.
The sooty bridge that hid it's gyen 'n' aall.
Aa wonder if Ma Faddon's singin' now

77

roond some Ower Sixties' piana,
makin' merry wi' the Age Concern.
Or is she, leyk a geet grey bass,
blood tricklin' doon from lip 'n' gill,
deed! Wi' them goggly eyes aall flattened oot 'n' dry?
Heather Harrison

You might wish to link this work to Unit 7 of *On and Off the Record*.

Page 101

For the second option I think I would want one student to act as advocate for each of the dub poems, presenting first the poem then the case for the poem: why in his eyes it is the strongest protest. The class might discuss what techniques in poetry appear to be most effective in communicating strong feelings. Because they are writing performance poetry, the process of drafting will require trial performances, so that there can be reworking as a consequence of audience reaction. In this context, class evaluation of students' work will be part of the process of composition. A group of your students might, at this point, wish to work through *Agony Column*.

Page 102/103

You might want to use these activities one by one as warm-up activities at the start of lessons or as material for a relaxing session after a sequence of demanding work. In this case I think you would perhaps act as master of ceremonies, bringing in students to 'perform' each section for the class, moving about the room to involve everyone and generally orchestrating a lively hour session. The last three options would require more circumspection and could be offered separately.
A group of your students could do an extended piece of research during homework and lesson time into the local dialect, writing up their findings in one of the ways suggested on Repromaster 35.

Unit 6
Page 112/113

I'd use the graffiti board for a display of phrases with the word 'man' and the word 'woman' in, and later do the same for phrases with 'black' or 'white' in. I would feed in poems selected from *Yesterday, Today and Tomorrow* published by NATE, and I would finish the work on this page by asking students to discuss in groups what might be done about sexism and racism in the language itself. The same groups could discuss the extract from *Of Mice and Men* and the question of what their policy would be regarding such books if they were English teachers. The discursive piece at the bottom of this page would have to be prepared carefully by the students with brainstorming of ideas, shaping, roughing out a draft, checking through with a partner and reworking.

Page 114/115

You might want to take the class through these two pages, discussing the quotations before letting them choose which of the options they would like to do. You might link this work with Units 4 and 5 of *On and Off the Record*, and a group might begin work on the Investigation Unit *Campaign*. On the wall you could have an 'active display' of headlines found by the students for which others would write stories for particular newspapers.

Page 116/117

You could develop the work on euphemism if you wished by linking with Unit 6 of *On and Off the Record*. I would take the class through the work, discussing the poem and the extract, then ask the students to choose the option they wished to do. I'd be inclined only to share the conversation in which the sensitive word was not to be mentioned, reminding students of the *Fawlty Towers* sketch in which John Cleese was determined not to mention the war.

Page 118/119

I'd want to ask the students to consider the gestures of the teachers in the school, local preachers and their own classmates and to analyse them. What was a particular teacher's style, for example? Was it helpful to the communication of her meaning? Are there certain gestures used by students in the school which are used by a particular cult or movement? Why do people use them?

Page 121

The assignments on this page are very demanding. You will probably want the students to do all of them and do them thoroughly. I would introduce two novels on the theme of protest against nuclear power: *Monster in Our*

79

Midst by Peggy Woodford and *The Guilty Party* by Joan Lingard. I would probably read one or two extracts and hope that two students would want to read them and report back to the class. It would be useful to know in this context what were their comparative strengths and what particular strategies and arguments were used by the protagonists. A group of students might wish to work on **Agony Column**.

Page 124/125

I would have a group of students making a thorough survey of the locality for graffiti during homework and lesson time. This group would not be expected to bring back particularly lurid examples but would attempt to carry out a serious investigation, the results of which they would present to the whole class. During this work the graffiti board would probably prove inadequate for the amount of material for display so I would give over more space temporarily. I would have two small groups working on improvisations and the rest of the students on written work. We would finish by sharing our work.

SEVERAL STORIES HIGH

Unit 1
Page 6

You might have favourite novels in which the author talks about the nature of story that you would want to use alongside the first section. I think I would use a few extracts from *Waterland* by Graham Swift to prompt the students as a class to have an open discussion on the subject. Then, to get things going right away, with the students still all working together, I'd have a few of the sort of story-making games that are used in radio parlour games. The class could be divided into two teams which would have to tell stories in turn
• to which each student contributed one sentence beginning with the next letter of the alphabet;
• which included a given six unconnected nouns;
• which had a particular beginning and end;
• with a particular title;
• taken up immediately by another member of the team whenever a bell was rung;
• which changed genre or voice or atmosphere when the bell was rung;
• which became very descriptive where the bell was rung ...

Page 8

The introduction to *The End of Enoch?* by Alan Sillitoe, mentioned in **Agony Column**, is interesting on how stories are written.

Page 9

This is a difficult section which I would be inclined to take the students through myself, reading the passages to them and helping them talk them out.

Page 11

The options might be shared between eight groups with a presentation session when they have been completed. The first option could lead to a group doing extended work on the Investigation Unit **Comedy & Humour**, if you felt the time was right. Alternatively the 'six good reasons' for telling stories could be shared between six groups who would work on their sections until completion then present the work to the rest of the class.

Page 14

If on a Winter's Night a Traveller ought to be read to the class, after careful preparation. Repromaster 3 helps with the difficulties of the text. The questions for discussion and improvisations on page 17 and the paired work and writing options on page 18 are a quick and varied interlude before the second extract from this book.

Page 20

Last lines of books, like famous people's last words, would make an interesting subject for the graffiti board. I think I would want to feed in *The Widow's Son*, the short story by Mary Lavin, at this point. It can be found in *Stories*, edited by Jackson and Pepper and published by Penguin, and uses two distinct endings to very good effect. It would be a helpful introduction to the more demanding work in Endings.

Page 22

You might want six students to begin work on *Opening Up the Airwaves* after group work on the options.

Page 24

There is work on advertising in other *Initiatives* books that you might want to use alongside this material. Have a look at the poems quoted on the last two pages of *Roots &Routes* and the third section of *The Right Idea* which looks at the subject in detail.

Page 27

A lot of attention is paid to the nature of photographs, at the beginning of *On and Off the Record* particularly and, to some extent, in *The Right Idea*.

Unit 2
Page 30

The tape recording of people of different ages telling the same story is such a good homework activity for students working in pairs that it is a pity that the whole class can't be involved. It is most unlikely, though, that you would have enough tape recorders for all the students to do it at the same time and, even if you had, organising the classroom for the playbacks and transcriptions would be an impossibility. It might be worth arranging for groups of students to do the activity in turn throughout the term, but there are other similar tasks in the *Initiatives* books, and I would be inclined to put them up for grabs as they occurred. In this case I think I would present the six tasks on this page as options so that the six or eight students doing the taping and the group working on an improvisation could be accommodated without causing undue distraction. The group doing Interweaving a Story (Repromaster 10) should work in pairs, comparing versions on completion.

Page 31   I'd organise the class into pairs for this activity.

Page 32/33   As teacher I would be inclined to take the students through all the material on this page, then ask them to form three groups. Each group would do the three activities but in a different order from the others. The whole class, working in pairs, could do Repromaster 11, Grave Fascination.

The collection of epitaphs would make a very good homework, or a whole class visit if there is a graveyard close to the school. Epitaphs might be a subject for the graffiti board.

Page 34/37   I'd take the class through these extracts and use the questions as the basis of a full class discussion.

Page 38/39   You might want to have different groups of students working on the activity of their choice. It would be interesting to compare the work done by one group doing an improvisation with the help of a student-director with that of another without one. The work produced in the Restructuring Stories activity could form an 'active learning display' in that students could be invited to write beside it which version they preferred, with reasons.

Page 40   As preparation for the homework I should play the tape to the whole class and work carefully through the transcript. Unless you do this, several of the students will probably 'forget' their homework. In any case, some probably will, so you will have to be prepared for them to continue with the radio presentation.

Page 41   The feedback from the rest of the class after any of the improvisations should be helpful in improving and developing the plots so that the next activity in the sequence will be more successful.

Page 42   Note the warning at the end of the group writing section! Students can be doing the Suggestions section at the same time.

Page 43/44	I think you will need to talk the students through this activity very carefully, though you will probably have students in the class who are very familiar with adventure game books, in which case they will be able to explain how they work, and how they can be written, to the rest. The resulting books should be made to look as attractive and finished as possible – the Art department might be able to help – and they should be given to read to various people who will provide useful feedback. You might want some of your students to conduct an age-based survey in the school to discover who likes them and why.
Page 45/46	There are five discrete activities here. You could have your class as a whole working through all of them or, perhaps better, five groups each working on a different one and sharing their work at the end. It is important for the results of any survey to be discussed fully, not only from the point of view of what has been found out but also how valid the survey method was. By this means you might be able to increase the validity of your students' surveys.

Unit 3
Page 48

I think I'd expect some of the students to want to try writing stories like those of Bob Taylor, and if they did I'd give them the opportunity.

Page 50/51	I'd have the students working in pairs right through this unit.
Page 54	With the class in a circle I would ask for volunteers to play the parts of the characters, responding to advice from the floor. I'd use this to set off the following three optional activities.
Page 55/57	The full class could be taken through a reading of the extracts from Ursula Le Guin's short story with pairs of students working on the questions as they occur. When the reading journals have been completed they could be displayed to provide models for other students to follow if they wished.
Page 60	Before asking students in groups to choose one of the four

options on page 60 I would want to spend some time helping them in pairs to analyse the language of the passages by Eldridge and Kafka, exploring how they were getting their effects. The paired work supported by my interventions would lead to a brief full class discussion.

Page 63/65

A stimulating link might be made between the story of Zeynel and Unit 2 of *On and Off the Record*, which looks at the 'legends' of Dick Turpin, Marilyn Monroe and Winnie Mandela; though a link might be made instead when you deal with Unit 5 in *Several Stories High* which looks at myths and legends. Because the text of *The Sea-Crossed Fisherman* is difficult I think I'd read it to the class.

Page 66/67

I would divide up the class with eight students (2 x 4) involved in the first option, four in the second, four in the work on the two fragments, six (2 x 3) in the work on the play fragment, four (2 x 2) on the penultimate and four (2 x 2) on the last. This final one, incidentally, is very hard to do and requires a lot of self-discipline on the part of the students, otherwise the conventions enabling it to work and the timing will go wrong. When they have been thoroughly prepared, each group should present its work to the rest of the students, who can share this experience of story and evaluate the preparation process, the presentations themselves and what has been learnt.

Page 70

I think I'd encourage some students to consider writing a scene or two for a play that used the convention of narrator. A look at the device in Robert Bolt's *A Man for All Seasons* might be useful at this point.
Before leaving this unit I'd reinforce students' growing understanding of how the author has power to shape her story by inviting them to write their own story in which either
•the crisis is a tiny incident around which the characters in their different ways reveal themselves; or
•the main character dies at a crucial stage; or
•an unexpected visitor changes the course of the story; or
•the outcome is affected by a letter not arriving at its destination; or
•the main character is not who she appeared to be.

I'd also like to give them the chance to investigate the way some pop or folk balladeers manage to write a story using very few words, and write themselves in this succinct and resonant way.

Unit 4

I'd take the full class fairly carefully through the plot synopsis of *Measure for Measure* and Tennyson's *Mariana* dealing with the questions orally, then ask each group of students to choose one of the options (page 74) and present their finished work to the class.

Page 77

The collection of pictures etc. would make a good homework ...

Page 78

... or a picture hanging somewhere in the classroom or about the school, or one of yours' or the students' ...

Page 81

I'd ask the students to work in pairs to explore the background to *An Autumn Story*. They would find Repromaster 20 very helpful for the second option.

Page 82

Geoffrey Holloway's poem deserves time spent on it. So does Liz Loxley's. I would ask the students to choose one or other and learn as much of it as they could for homework. I'd ask them in pairs to choose one verse of *Charades: September* until all the verses were chosen (twenty students/ten verses) and make a collage (3D if it were that time of year) of their verse. This would produce a frieze of the poem which could be displayed.

Page 84/85

Pairs of students would do this work, and you could give them the option of continuing their work through Repromasters 21, 22a and 22b.

Page 86

I'd represent the 'busy social life in the courtyard' by having the whole class involved but at first forming tableaux, silent and motionless groups which I would bring to life one at a time until each was performing well. Then I'd bring them all in together. Frequent pauses for reflection and further discussion would lead eventually to a convincing scene.

Page 88	You will have your own favourite passages for use alongside the James. Leon Garfield takes some beating, and Dickens of course.

Page 90/91

I'd want to pause here for a full class discussion on how possible it is to represent a smell or a taste with words. I would feed in Ted Hughes' concern to catch the essence of an animal or bird, 'the crowiness of a crow'. I'd try to draw out from the students ideas like
• comparisons – similes and metaphors;
• lists of comparisons;
• carefully chosen words – nouns, verbs, adjectives;
• anecdotes;
• contrasts and juxtapositions;
• precise use of words;
• a sudden change of style;
then take them through the second section from *Sequins for a Ragged Hem* and ask them to consider how Amryl Johnson does it.

Page 92

If the school owns a video it would be very worthwhile for a group to make their own pop video expressing the theme or atmosphere of a current lyric.
You might want to conclude this unit by asking the students at first in groups to take one of the passages they have been looking at and
• find words for how the passage makes them feel;
• try to explain how the author makes this effect.

Unit 5

Before students work in groups on the differences between myths, legends and story you will need to talk the issue through with the whole class. You might also want to feed in your own material. Robert Frost's poem *After Apple Picking* comes to mind as useful at this time and later in the unit when you might want to encourage your students to think about image and symbol and allegory. These concepts might be played around with here but developed further in connection with the material on the sea (pages 102/103).

Page 98

It would be a worthwhile homework for students to tape a grandparent, parent and teenager retelling the same well-

known story, transcribe the recordings and study them for their differences. If several students were to do this, the cross-checking of similarities and differences might produce some interesting points. To investigate how a story would change depending on the age of the audience would also throw up interesting ideas.

Time should be given for preparation before telling the stories and an attempt made after each one by the class to draw up a list of criteria for what makes a successful oral storytelling. You might want students to tape some of these stories, write their stories, transcribe their oral stories and compare the two versions to see what the differences are. This might be a way of investigating how oral and written language are different in their natures.

Page 100

I would distribute one of the eight discussion points to each of eight small groups of three or four students. Responses should be shared with the full class for further discussion.

Page 101

You might want to give your students the opportunity to explore this excellent material further by
• setting one or other to music and performing it;
• writing their own versions;
• discussing their emotional response to each verse;
• writing to Julie Fullarton about the legend and her versions.
After playing the tape of Sam McAughtry telling his story while the students follow the text on Repromaster 28a, I would divide them into three groups, one for discussion, one for drama and one for writing activities as described on Repromaster 28b. We would share the work when it was finished.

Page 103

Your students could have the opportunity here to refine their criteria for good oral storytelling, and the opportunity would be enhanced if a storyteller were engaged to come and give a performance to your class. One of your students could, perhaps, make the arrangements for Julie Fullarton herself, Grace Hallworth, Beulah Candappa or Lennie Alsopp, all of whom have myths in their repertoire, to come for a session. They would all be interested in talking about the material itself and the art of storytelling.

Page 105

You will need to prepare for the Research Into Legends by either forewarning the central library of a possible influx of students or getting into the school a large collection of books on the subject. If it is to be a satisfactory number and range of books to accommodate the needs of the whole class your central librarian will probably need a few weeks' warning so that she can acquire the stock. On the other hand you may prefer to have only a small number of students on this activity. I would be interested in getting some to try writing ballad versions of stories that particularly appealed to them.

Page 107

For the option of developing a myth on a local landmark to work satisfactorily some research by students should take place to establish the nature of these stories. Perhaps a small group could be sent to the library to make investigations and on their return, as experts, tell the rest of the class what they had found out. Then, after discussions about appropriate sites and making sure not to be too derivative, writing could start.

Page 109

I would take the whole class fairly briskly through these questions, then dwell on the writing task, perhaps using material from the Investigations Unit *Other Worlds* to help establish the nature of the science fiction genre with the students.

Page 110/113

Links could also be made here, in this case with *The Right Idea*, Unit 1. Students would probably find the interplay of approaches useful to them. It might be useful, too, to liaise with the Art teacher in case she could join your class for a while to offer her thoughts.

Page 114

I would put Steinbeck's description of Slim when he first appears in *Of Mice and Men* alongside Heroes and the Media. It is a short but definitive introduction to the hero figure in this book.

Page 115

It would be a pity not to finish this unit with a

comprehensive display including extended writing, artwork and a performance of students' ballads and poetry set to music. It could be used to tell another class or another year about myth and legend.

Unit 6
Page 118/119

This research, which you would probably set for homework, could lead to the production of some remarkable material, particularly if the student already has a close affinity for a grandparent or more distant relation or discovers an ancestor who particularly interests him. Before beginning to write the narrative it would be useful for each student to work for a while with another, talking through material and possible approaches to it.

Page 120/121

There might be students in your class who can add to 'the words and phrases used by the Caribbean woman'. In any case, there will be the opportunity for your students as a class to begin to explore the use of equivalent phrases in various dialects and perhaps for a group which becomes particularly interested in the subject of dialectal phrases to take the research further.
Snatches of conversation might be collected over several weeks and either kept in a journal or written up on the graffiti board so that the class as a whole can discuss them. The special qualities that 'ordinary language' has should be identified if possible.
Your students might find the dramatic scene easier to write if their characters are based on people they know well who would use the kind of language that they have collected.

Page 122/123

I would divide the class into groups of four and give one of the briefs to each. Two students in each group should take the parts suggested and the other two advise them. Each finished piece should be performed in turn and the rest of the class be invited to discuss it carefully from the point of view of its quality as a presentation and its context.

Page 125

Creating Family Documentation is a good opportunity for an 'active display' – the story told through documentation and displayed on the classroom wall would be the basis on which other students could create an oral story.

Page 126/127

You could take the whole class through *The Mayor of Casterbridge* and the *Mansfield Park* extracts. Then half the class in groups of four (two acting, two advising) could do the role play and the other half the discussion, spending time also looking at how the issues are skirted round in the language itself.

Page 128/129

This could turn out to be a very rich field. You may have your own source of old letters. Some of your students might have access to a hoard. Good examples can be extremely intriguing and could prompt some very enthusiastic work. You might want to offer some other specific examples of how your students might tackle the Story by Letter assignment:

•letters which reveal unrequited love, or secret feelings or fears;
•letters which reveal the plotting behind a public event;
•letters which disclose one side of the story only;
•letters between friends who have never met;
•letters between two people, one of whom has a guilty secret;
•letters from a prisoner, or a hospital patient, or someone in boarding school;
•letters between characters from legend.

Page 133

For the Creating Atmosphere activity I would have the class working in two large groups. Within each group I would have students working in pairs on each task, occasionally meeting together with the rest of the group to ensure that the project was gelling. Adjustments would have to be made when they met to discuss progress, unless they were able to keep fairly close contact throughout. All this work would result in two large displays, each of which could be presented to the other group by a team of students or by one student who might have had the director's role throughout.

Page 134

The central project of the Family Tree section is the writing of a family saga. Some students would find it easier and more satisfying to work on their own while others would prefer to work as part of a team, perhaps concentrating on one or two episodes within the grand design. They might be helped somewhat if you gave them a breakdown of the family trees and timescale of a Russian or a South American novel like *One Hundred Years of Solitude* or *The House of the Spirits*.

You will need to be prepared for some students wishing to write at length and over a considerable time in this project, and if your students intend their completed books to be kept in the school or class library they will perhaps want to use word processors and bind them attractively.

INVESTIGATION UNITS

There are five Investigation Units: *Agony Column,
Campaign, Comedy & Humour, Opening Up the Airwaves*
and *Other Worlds*. They take as their theme language in
use: the potential of language in various situations; the
way we can use the language to express our concerns,
persuade others to change their mind, make others laugh
or cringe or cry. The approach is genuinely investigative
so that students can explore an aspect of language, usually
with a classmate, and bring back real information which
can be shared with the rest of the class. Because the
subject matter is firmly based in the real world, there is a
strong tendency for this language-based work to develop
a cross-curricular dimension.

The Investigation Units start with a few brief introductory
activities and move into longer and more demanding
investigations. The usual pattern is general description of
the subject area, common focus work, a series of options
requiring lengthy research work, presentations and a
review of what has been accomplished. Often the Unit is
concluded with a list of optional further activities.

The element of choice is found throughout the Units. Even
if you decide to use them with the whole class you will
find a great deal of opportunity for student choice in the
way the work is presented. At times you may decide that
you will select six students whom you would like to work
together on a Unit. It is important from the point of view
of providing a real audience for the work as well as
keeping groups firmly integrated into the main class that
work is periodically fed back to the class and that
completed work is properly presented.

As teacher, you will need to
• decide when it is appropriate for a group to work on an
Investigation Unit;
• decide on the composition of that group;
• decide whether work should be done
  − all in the classroom
  − in the school library
  − in another subject teacher's classroom
  − about the school in break times
  − about the school in lesson times
  − after school and at weekends in the community
  − out of school in lesson times;

- support the work of the group by
  - working alongside them as individuals and as a group
  - ensuring that Repromasters can be readily copied
  - helping make cross-curricular links
  - helping with arrangements should experts be required to visit or members of the group wish to leave the classroom during lesson time or the premises during school time
  - creating the conditions necessary for the production of high quality work
  - finding a range of suitable audiences to receive the work.

Some of the Investigation Units are textually more demanding than others, though all are accessible to the average mixed ability group. You will need to know the material well though, so that you can quickly provide clarification or advice if required.

AGONY COLUMN

This Unit should be accessible to all of your students. It begins with discussion work and letter writing in role, and is concerned throughout with feelings and the effective expression of feelings.

Page 5-11

For the Purpose and Choice Alternative 1, students will need to talk through with you who they should interview and when. Advice on drawing up questionnaires and carrying out surveys can be found in *Opening Up the Airwaves* (page 7). For Alternative 3 students will either have to make video or audio recordings for homework or borrow recordings from the school or local library.

Page 33

The End of Enoch? can be found in *Men, Women and Children*, a collection of short stories written by Alan Sillitoe and published by Star Books. The author gives his reasons for writing the sequel in a short preface which your students might find useful in their work on how writers write.

Page 38

Students doing the Communicatingthe Message alternative might need to use a telephone, in which case you will need to make this possible beforehand.
The preparation of broadsheets is a major piece of work, possibly requiring assistance from the Art or Technology departments. If cameras are scarce in the school you may have to ask for capitation to buy one or two or ask students if they can provide their own.

Page 40

The debate is an optional activity. If your students want to contact an expert, give them your advice, let them make the necessary arrangements and keep an eye on developments. A big debate involving more than one class would be stimulating.

Page 42

There is another version of this poem containing an additional three verses which appears, for example, in *The English Auden: Poems, Essays and Dramatic Writings 1927-1939*. If your students are able to find it they might like to discuss whether or not, as editors, they would wish to include them if they were publishing the poem.

For the first alternative it is likely that students will need to visit the town library. They may wish to borrow recordings from members of staff, visit the local folk club or invite an expert in for discussion or a performance. It is probable that they will need help in making contacts. For the second alternative they will probably need considerable help from you.

The sharing and the evaluation should be done thoroughly.

CAMPAIGN

This Unit is demanding and will require careful reading by your students, but the material has an engaging immediacy and the main activity is role play on the theme of persuasion, so they will quickly become involved in the work. Unless you have a student acting as manager of the Repromasters you will have to take this role yourself. He or you should become thoroughly familiar with the material, should sort out the role cards beforehand and issue each member of the group with a folder in which work in progress can be kept. Links with the Art or Technology department might be helpful.

Page 11   It would help students at this point if they were to draw on their own experience, comparing anything that had happened or was happening in their locality of a similar nature to the Langdell Valley development.

Page 12   The decision as to whether the group is for or against the development is crucial. It should only be taken after all the arguments have been rehearsed. It will have a direct bearing on the rest of the work in the Unit.

Page 14/15   This is the second point where your students need to be very clear as to what is expected of them. After as much discussion time as they find necessary they should decide (i) what will be the group's main campaign event; and (ii) which alternative media activity each pair will do. (Any pair finishing before the others could do a second activity.)

Page 16   This page, on ethics, should be discussed fully with reference to the students' own experiences and perceptions.

Page 20   This section on using tape recorder and microphone is useful throughout *Initiatives*.

Page 23   You might have some examples of formal letters to hand for this section.

Page 25   There is very helpful advice here on print.

Page 27	To make a video would certainly give this work more purpose. If the school does not possess the necessary equipment perhaps it could be borrowed from the Teachers' Centre.
Page 30	Perhaps a member of the local press might visit as an expert at this point.
Page 32	There is very good advice here on how to write a press release.
Page 37/38	There is very useful advice here and on Repromasters 13 and 14 on pre-interview questions and preparing for an interview.
Page 40	If there is time, the group might want to do this optional extra.
Page 41/42	There are clear instructions here on how a group might make its presentation.
	Advice on Repromasters 8, 11 and 12 should be carefully read by the students, as appropriate.

COMEDY AND HUMOUR

This Unit should be accessible to all your students. It begins with general work on what we laugh at and why.

Page 7

Here is useful advice on how students can work effectively in pairs.

Page 8

Your students may need help with how to conduct a survey (page 7 of *Opening up the Airwaves*).

Page 14

Your students will need to read this page extremely carefully and talk it through to make sure they have fully understood the directions. Each student should read through all the alternatives to get a clear overview of the subject before getting down to paired work on the topics chosen.

Page 15-30

Each alternative has two parts to it, the investigation itself and a related production. You may wish your students to link up with the Art or Technology departments for some of this work. Some students will need recordings taken from the television or radio, which could be done for homework if they or a friend have the machinery.

Page 33

Students might be able to arrange for local experts to come in to talk about the subject, and they can record examples of ethnic jokes from the radio and television. Rabbi Lionel Blue would be a good subject. But to make a collection of jokes involving different nationalities or from different countries, students will need to spend homework time interviewing classmates and their families from different countries of origin and researching in the community.

Page 34

Material can be collected from older members of the students' families on the issue of whether or not humour dates, but it would be an interesting use of homework time for students to visit a local old people's home to record examples from the residents and bring their material back to the classroom for analysis.

Page 37

The work should be rounded off with a presentation to the classroom on the nature of humour, involving examples of various forms of comedy and related information. If it were successful it should be presented to a wider, more public audience.

OPENING UP THE AIRWAVES

Beginning with research on people's listening habits and preferences, this Unit goes on to describe five different types of radio station. Students choose one of these types and plan programmes appropriate to it.

Page 7

The guidelines for drawing up a questionnaire are extremely useful. Some students will probably want to do a survey of people in the community, which could be conducted in homework or class time.

Page 10

This is the introduction to various kinds of radio stations. Students should read through all the material and do the incidental short activities. The section on schools radio (page 21) may prompt investigation into their own school facilities or into the practice of neighbouring schools, in which case a visit might be appropriate.

Page 22

Here are the instructions for the next stage of the work.

Page 27

Here is the introduction to the main piece of work in the Unit, the establishment of the groups' own radio station, modelled on one of the types of station just investigated.

Page 29

These are important instructions for the next sequence of work. Five alternatives are listed from which students in pairs should select one: the group should ensure that at least two are covered. You will need to ensure that a tape recorder, microphone and blank tapes are available.

Page 36

The ideal would be for the finished programme to go out on the school radio and, failing that, on any in-house broadcasting system. Your students might be able to arrange for another school to broadcast the programme. It might well be, though, that you will have to arrange for the programmes to be played on a tape recorder to a specific audience, in which case every effort should be made to ensure a good presentation.

Advice on Repromasters 10, 11, 12 and 13 should be read thoroughly by your students, as appropriate.

OTHER WORLDS

Pages 9 and 13

Although this is textually a demanding Unit it should be accessible to the average mixed ability group: the introductory activities are appealing, the structure is clear and the alternatives are imaginative and varied. You might find it useful to prepare a member of the Science department for possible approaches from members of the group keen to give their work authenticity. You will probably want to build up a large and wide-ranging display of science fiction in your classroom to act as a backdrop and a resource for the work in this Unit.

Page 14

Page 41

Your students may wish to interview people in the community about attitudes to and tastes in science fiction, in which case you have to decide when would be the best time for them to do it.

Page 42

This is where the way of working is described:
- the group should cover six of the seven alternatives
- students should work in pairs, collaboratively
- each pair should complete two alternatives
- the alternatives should be done in sequence.

When all this work has been completed, the group should plan a presentation on the genre of science fiction for the class, which, if successful, should be given to a wider, more public audience.

Two further alternatives are described here, both involving a great deal of work and requiring your support. It is particularly the organisation of the scriptwriting that you will need to advise on.

The information and advice about interviewing technique on Repromasters 1a, 1b, 2a, 2b and 3 should be read thoroughly by your students, as appropriate.

PART II

CHAPTER ONE

THE CLASSROOM

Many English teachers lead very good sessions in Chemistry laboratories where English resources are not to hand, students' English work is not displayed and the furniture cannot be arranged in an appropriate manner. They make the best of a bad job by bringing material they expect to need with them, negotiating for display space on one wall and by encouraging their students to work in twos or threes as they sit side by side along their benches. This chapter argues that such conditions are not satisfactory for English sessions, makes a case for specialist English accommodation and describes how such accommodation might be utilised.

Learning
The Right Frame of Mind

Over Christmas I was challenged by my stepfather to a game of chess, a game that I play badly. Although he had always beaten me before without much effort he seemed to expect a long tussle and his serious approach to the game made me play with more belief in myself than usual. I played carefully and deliberately and, surprisingly, I won. I felt so pleased with myself that for the next few days I could have tackled anything.

This - unfortunately transitory - feeling reminded me of a scene from Virginia Mae Axline's *Dibbs: in Search of Self* where Dibbs's lesson with his remedial teacher is interrupted by the Head. Dibbs's teacher politely but firmly asks the Head to come back at the end of the lesson: he is busy at the moment with something very important and cannot be disturbed. "Important?" thinks Dibbs. "Me, Important?" And from that moment begins Dibbs's rehabilitation as a learner.

People say that if you take up an instrument in later life you crave to be asked by your music teacher to play a tune that you have mastered. You need the opportunity to show that you are not always clumsy, slow and inept. You need to find security in the achievement you have already gained. And you need praise, warm and frequent.

Learning

As teachers, we have to consider, above all, the nature of the learning process. We have to be alert to how we learn and how others learn so that we can apply our insights to our practice in the classroom. If I can play a better game of chess because I know a good player takes my challenge seriously, if Dibbs starts to improve when he senses that his teacher values his sessions with him, then we, learning from our experience and our reading, should ensure that our students are keenly aware of our interest and confidence in them as learners. If the student is to apply himself confidently and purposefully he needs to feel capable, potentially able to do the job in hand; he needs, at least in the early stages, to feel that his successes are being recognised and enjoyed by the teacher and by other students. The learning transaction is a very delicate affair in which a sense of failure, a lack of confidence, can drain away the energy or concentration necessary for a task to be done to anything like the level of which a student is capable.

Teaching is such a difficult craft that we need to see ourselves all the time as learners, and we can improve ourselves as teachers by reflecting on how we learn.

We will learn, too, by observation of other teachers in their classrooms, department colleagues and teachers in other schools, particularly if our attention is mainly focused not on the teachers but on the behaviour of the students. Teachers often work so hard in a lesson that they are exhausted by the end of the afternoon, yet their students may be doing very little; their contribution, being strongly teacher-directed, can be desultory and spasmodic. But strategies can be found which commit the class to a variety of activities and release the teacher to do the more effective work of
•stimulating;
•challenging;
•prompting;
•questioning;
•directing;
•extending;
•supporting;
•responding to
each individual or group as required.

arning Through iscussion

We can learn a great deal about how our students learn by the analysis of tape recordings of their discussions.

Recently, I made a tape of four eleven year-old children discussing *Green Man in the Garden* by Charles Causley:

Green Man in the Garden

Green Man in the garden
   Staring from the tree,
Why do you look so long and hard
   Through the pane at me?

Your eyes are dark as holly
   Of sycamore your horns,
Your bones are made of elder-branch,
   Your teeth are made of thorns.

Your hat is made of ivy-leaf,
   Of bark your dancing shoes,
And evergreen and green and green
   Your jacket and shirt and trews.

Leave your house and leave your land
   And throw away the key,
And never look behind, he creaked,
   And come and live with me.

I bolted up the window,
   I bolted up the door,
I drew the blind that I should find
   The green man never more.

But when I softly turned the stair
   As I went up to bed,
I saw the green man standing there,
   Sleep well, my friend, he said.

   I read the poem to a mixed ability group of children and asked them to discuss for an hour how they would illustrate it. Then I left the room and returned at the end of the session to find them still deep in discussion. Here is a transcript taken from towards the end of the session:

Chris: ... Well I don't think that man or boy would sleep well if that green man was watching him.

106

John: Yeah that's a good time for music.

Sarah: No, because it does say that, see it just ends with 'Sleep well, my friend, he said', and then he probably disappeared.

Chris: I wonder if he wants a friend with him in the end?

Sarah: Yeah, and he probably disappeared.

Chris: Because he's saying 'my friend, he said'. He'd say 'my enemy', if he ...

Sarah: No he wouldn't say that.

John: He wouldn't say 'my enemy'. He'd say 'my ... '

Martin: He might.

Sarah: 'Sleep well, my enemy'.

Martin: He wouldn't say 'Sleep well, my enemy'.

John: Might not be saying it as in you know pout?

Chris: Why would he come and live with him if he didn't want him? If he didn't like him why would he want him to come ... be lonely ... He must want him to come, must like him.

Sarah: Perhaps he's lonely and wants him to turn into a treeman himself.

John: Maybe he was killed somehow, and he just wants him to be with him or maybe he wants to punish him or something.

Chris: He said 'my friend', so he's not in the mood to punish him is he?

Martin: He wants to punish him. No, he might be ... acting sort of thing, acting.

John: But he might be sort of laughing. He might be laughing behind his ... voice.

Chris: He could be mocking him saying 'Sleep well, sleep well, huh! I've got something coming tomorrow' or something.

Martin: Yeah.

I like this for many reasons, but particularly because you can experience their gradual construction, through "Might not be saying it as in you know pout", and "He might be laughing behind his voice" to "He could be mocking", of an understanding of irony. Having tried to get classes of top set eleventh year students to relate to Jane Austen's use of irony and failed, I find this achievement on the part of four mixed ability eleven year-old children remarkable. They weren't used to this sort of learning in the classroom either, and the teacher (me) was drinking coffee in the staffroom whilst this was going on!

Ownership

This short transcript reveals the tremendous, often unacknowledged, capabilities that the students themselves bring to school. Often they are sponges, soaking up the teacher's knowledge; often they are not given the scope to use their own language skills or draw on their own unique and profound experience for
•their stories;
•their arguments;
•their opinions and
•their wisdom.
Their world of beliefs, tastes, attitudes, interests can be neglected: their feelings can be undervalued, their self-expression neglected. The student who has learned and experienced so much out of school without recourse to complex structures and systems is sometimes crushed by steamrollering curricula, externally determined targets and too much didactic teaching.

We can easily forget, in the throes of board of studies or department meetings, that the student as learner should be at the forefront of all our thinking about education. We can get so caught up with administration and routines that we fail to keep the particular needs of the student at the top of our agenda. And, even in our lessons, the experience of each student is not always highly regarded, is sometimes neglected and undervalued, so that the work we set can appear to them irrelevant, pointless or undemanding.

All students need the chance
•to think, talk and write in such ways that more sense can be made of who they are and what is happening to them, of their relationships and the behaviour of others;
•to exercise their remarkable language capabilities in the expression of their feelings and opinions in stories and arguments;
•to learn that they can influence events through their powers of speech and writing.
They should not have to suffer the demoralising effect

• of being told that they are not very good at using their own language;
• of being led to believe that their dialect is inferior to Standard English;
• of being given second rate material to work with or easy tasks to complete because the teacher does not expect much from them;
• of being treated as empty vessels to be filled with the wisdom of others.

Ourselves as Language Users

A great deal is now known about language acquisition and development and the English teacher needs to keep abreast of this new knowledge. But it is crucial for reading about how our ability with language develops to be backed up by practice in talking and writing, so that we can experience for ourselves how in different circumstances we formulate and shape our expression. We need to identify from our own behaviour the importance of self-confidence to our oral performance. John was only able to help the group he was part of to reach an understanding about irony by having the self-possession to grope aloud for meanings he could scarcely grasp himself. Because he felt able to take the risk he seems to have found words that have brought him a new understanding. And, ironically, it is unlikely that he would have found that confidence had the teacher been a member of the discussion group.

We need, too, to experience the tremendous difficulties, the minor successes, the sense of exposure that writing gives to know what it is like to be unable to continue a piece, to write with a better practitioner breathing down our neck or to have to read aloud to the class a piece that in our estimation is not what we meant at all. If we, as writers, know that the process of writing is very demanding but that only through writing can we become better writers, then we know, as teachers, that the writing of our students will only improve, become more subtle, more flexible, more fluent, through the act of writing. If the teacher is a writer who knows a certain amount about the language by reading about it and by writing with it, she is able to help the student in the act of writing by a finely judged

109

- suggestion;
- question;
- comparison;
- personal anecdote;
- encouraging comment.

The English teacher will tend to be a habitual reader of adult and children's fiction. The excitement she feels in generating her own language will be equally stimulated by the achievements of other writers. Nor could we stimulate a reluctant reader to pick up a book with serious intent to read it unless we have had experience of being moved to tears, of laughter or sadness, by our reading; unless we knew what it was like to stay up half the night to find the outcome of a well-told story and knew the strange pleasure of sitting safely on the edge of our seat in sheer suspense. There would be something fraudulent about the English teacher who urged her students to read and write but who herself did not have favourite passages and whole books, which she would at times reread with great pleasure, who did not have favourite authors whose new works were eagerly looked forward to.

If we are not frequently reading young adult fiction we will find ourselves at a loss to know what we might recommend to the student disinclined to read without guidance or the voracious reader needing a new lead. And the establishment of reading as a normal and frequent activity in and out of the classroom would be encouraged by the teacher seen reading herself.

A Supportive Department

It would be difficult to put as much effort into teaching English as these comments advocate unless considerable support was provided by a strong department. A teacher's high motivation and hard work depend on plenty of animated, informal discussion at break and lunchtimes about how lessons have gone and what minor and major successes have been achieved or observed.

Weekly department meetings can provide a semi-formal setting in which ideas can be shared and plans made:

- Some departments make sure that administration is covered in the first half hour so that the remaining hour is always given to matters more to do with the well-being of

110

the student as learner.

•Some plan their handbooks and schemes of work as a team, with some initially delegated responsibilities, but everything eventually talked through by all members together.

•Some make frequent use of outside speakers - specialist drama teachers, teacher-advisers, members of the National Curriculum Council or moderators for the GCSE Board - whose visits are an opportunity for short bursts of information followed by friendly but intense questioning.

•Some have a routine in which one book on English teaching is read by all the English teachers each term and the responsibility for leading a discussion on it is passed round the department.

This last means that a group of teachers in a fairly painless way can keep up-to-date on current language theory as a result of a slight pressure from the Head of Department, who buys the books out of capitation. Implicit, though, is the notion that a successful English teacher has to be committed full-time to this extremely demanding, exhilarating and exhausting job.

The Learning Environment
Specialist Accommodation

And just as the English student deserves to be taught by a specialist English teacher so he should be taught in specialist accommodation. We are concerned with the personal growth of this student of English, his emotional and intellectual growth, his sense of his own worth and the worth of his fellow beings, the development of his powers of communication and his appreciation of how others communicate to him. We are concerned, too, with the development of his aesthetic and his spiritual sense because these are areas of experience also developed in the context of the English lesson.

It is largely up to English teachers to provide the context for learning about the language, and this context of

•student-centred learning, in which personal experience is valued and personal expression and composition are studied, encouraged and developed;

•imaginative and sensitive response;

•delicate extension of the student's knowledge about the language;

•sophisticated student-student and teacher-student

111

interaction;
•informed tuition;
•resource-based learning, where what is needed will be at hand;

can really only be fully achieved in a specialist English classroom in which students feel confident, relaxed and stimulated.

It can be achieved to some extent, of course, in the Chemistry laboratory and, too often, it has to be; but managers of schools should be aware of the negative effect that non-specialist rooms and temporary classrooms have on their students' opportunities for learning. They should know that trying to teach English without a base can result in a lack of the necessary resources, harassed teachers and disaffected students. Moving from room to room or working in an inappropriate setting will make it harder for students to learn and tend to promote a didactic style of teaching. Temporary classrooms do have things to be said in their favour: they are generally light, they often have useful vestibules or cupboards, big enough to take a small group, and their isolation from other classrooms means that there is no problem with noise. That said, the proper place for the English classroom is in the main school, part of a suite of specialist rooms and fairly close to the school library and information centre.

The Ideal Classroom

It will be a light room, but with plenty of wall area for display boards. It will have shelves rather than cupboards, formica or wooden tables rather than desks. It will have a carpet on the floor to soften the general effect of the room and make the movement of students and furniture quieter: relationships with members of staff teaching on the floor below will be better if they are not frequently disturbed by chairs and tables scraping above their heads.

All rooms have drawbacks but also have possibilities that might have to be looked for and then exploited. If it is your own room you might bring in plants and objects related to the work in hand which will help to create a personal atmosphere; and a lick of paint over the walls once a year, done at the end of term with the help of some students with rollers, will give the room a freshness to help counteract gloomy winter weather.

If the tables are positioned round the edge of the room against the walls a wide and continuous work-surface can be achieved, and on this you can place dictionaries and thesauruses, one for each table. These reference books should always be at hand so that the students can use them whenever they need to.

As well as these there might be:
• a plastic box containing art materials: scissors, glue, charcoal, paint, crayons, felt tips, coloured and black card and stencils;
• a second containing lined and plain paper;
• a third with old colour magazines for collage work;
• a fourth containing the English Language and Literature coursework files; and
• a fifth containing ideas for individual and group activities.

It would also be good to see at least one computer/ word processor in every classroom, in a corner enclosed by a screen so that operators would not be distracted by or distract other members of the class.

Display

On the walls of the specialist English classroom there would be new and attractive displays of students' work. Some of the displays might be artistic responses to literature:
• 2D and 3D collages;
• silhouettes;
• friezes;
• posters;
• strip cartoons;
• diagrams;
• storyboards;
• drawings of main characters.

There might be mobiles hanging from the ceiling. There might be short pieces of writing:
• front pages of newspapers;
• copies of letters and the replies;
• work in progress;
• extracts from journals;
• poems;
• reviews;

•graffiti etc. (on the graffiti board).

There would be extended writing:
•longer stories;
•articles;
•magazines;
•reports on investigations;
•anthologies;

And there might be:
•drafts of pieces of work leading up to the fair copy;
•the whole text of a short novel or play being studied, the pages stuck one beside another in a large block, so that the students could trace out links of various sorts through the use of pins with coloured heads and thread.

It is worth spending time mounting students' work imaginatively so that the classroom looks inviting, the students can sense your appreciation of the worth of their work and people will view and read the exhibits; and the better a display is mounted the less chance there is of it being defaced.

When vandalism does occur the best response would seem to be to take the matter very seriously, draw attention to the fact that it is the students' own, very important work that is being ruined, and promptly replace the mutilated work with new material; and keep this up doggedly until the spoiling stops or the culprit is found.

There is a range of backing papers currently on the market – sugar papers, strongly coloured card, shiny and silver paper – any of which can contribute to making the English classroom a place in which students enjoy working. In fact, their sense of ownership would probably be increased if the responsibility to choose and mount the wall displays was theirs and if some of the displays invited an active response from them, with lists to be added to and clues to be answered.

Class Libraries

Every English room needs a class library, even if the school library is where it ought to be, just down the corridor. I don't mean a class library that is kept in a cardboard box, brought out of a cupboard or stored on cupboard shelves and unlocked once a week. Part of the value of the class library is simply that it can be seen, that

114

in the English classroom there are books about; plenty of new, attractive novels, poetry books and non-fiction that can be browsed through or borrowed at will.

The best container for a class library is probably the plastic-coated, wire frame sort that hangs on the wall and will display about a hundred books with their covers to the front so that all the texts are visible and accessible. It is not easy to throw away old and tatty copies but such squeamishness ought to be overcome so that only crisp and colourful books are on show. The message has to be that books are attractive and books are valued. If reading is important then we should not present our students with empty or no bookcases, or bookcases full of dun-coloured tat.

If the books are going to be alluring and readily available, some will inevitably go missing. Careful monitoring will cut down on losses, as will a page in an exercise book for each student with date of borrowing, book title and date of return, notes home and the occasional amnesty; but in the end if we are to give students the chance to read when they want to we have to accept that we will lose books, and it is better to lose a few books than to lock them away in the safety of a cupboard and try to teach English in a space that might as well be a changing room, or to spend precious money on lockable glazed cupboards for the price of which numerous books could be bought.

The book collection might be increased with
•books published by the students themselves;
•novels written by senior students for their juniors;
•school newspapers;
•school magazines;
•reports on research projects;
•thematic or project-based collections of writing;
•reports on surveys and questionnaires;
•local and national magazines;
•colour supplements;
•literary periodicals like *Signals* and *Books for Keeps*;
•syllabuses
and other reading matter.

The classroom might become a bookshop one or two lunchtimes each week.

A Thematic Display

In a corner of the room might be a display of reading material on a subject currently under study by one of the classes that use the room:
- a collection of cowboy or science fiction books;
- a collection of newspapers issued on the same day;
- a collection of myths or fairy stories;
- a collection of text books from another subject;
- anthologies of short stories;
- source books on a particular issue;
- works by a particular writer.

There might, instead, be a collection of fossils, or materials selected for their texture, their shape or their seasonal interest.

Source Books

Another shelving arrangement might carry source material of various kinds. There might be texts like *Initiatives* Investigation Units available for students to thumb through whenever they or the teacher wished, so that possibilities for future lessons could be explored. There might also be books
- of poems;
- about poetry;
- about words;
- of quotations;
- on slang;
- of common usage;
- of dialect;
- of history of the language;
- of follow-up material;
- of art and photography.

Tapes

It is here that the tape library could also be housed. There might be
- tapes of small group discussions for analysis and reference;
- tapes of authors reading their work;
- tapes made by students of local language behaviour;
- tapes of various classroom and extra-classroom activities still in progress;
- choral readings of poems;
- exemplar material to be used to model work on.

There might be a collection of videotapes too. Most of

the department's tapes would be centralised, but those made by students from the classroom and those particularly relevant to work in progress would be kept on these shelves.

Furniture Organisation
Model A

It·is revealing to watch a session in progress to see what an impact the arrangement of furniture makes to the learning process. Of the various organisational shapes Example A shows the model that is probably the most popular.

Example A

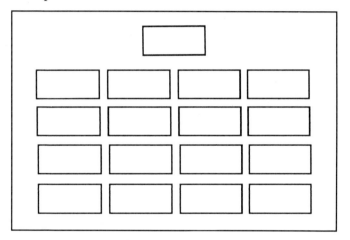

From the back of such a classroom an observer is struck by the way learning is dictated by the teacher. With her desk and the board at the front of the room, it suggests that every transaction of learning starts and finishes with her. Even in open class discussion when the teacher, promisingly enough, invites the students to compare, for example, two or three recently read short stories, it is inevitable that the teacher remains the physical focus of the 'conversation'. It is hard to achieve a genuine exchange of ideas between students when to look one's colleague in the eye means craning the neck and the risk of falling off one's chair. Unless there is a great deal of physical distortion, you talk to the back of a head, which does not ease social or linguistic interaction.

Co-operative learning by students in pairs is perfectly

possible in this arrangement but there is less flexibility, which could lead to a considerable amount of lecturing to the students, of students writing silently, sessions beginning with the teacher reading a short story or introducing a topic and ending with students writing their response in silence. There could be a tendency in such classrooms for the teacher to control the student's learning, for drafting to be uncommon, for all the students to start and finish the same activity at the same time, and for no more than the teacher's lip-service to be paid to the importance of talk in learning.

Model B

Because of the limitations of such a classroom arrangement many teachers arrange tables in pairs to make a layout that looks like Example B.

Example B

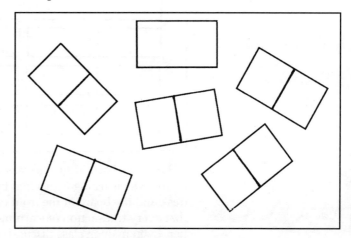

No longer is the teacher the focus of every activity. Group work is more common. Students sit around tables set together in pairs and they face each other, so the activities that grow naturally out of such an arrangement are small group discussion and co-operative project work. In Example B, students are given more status. They are invited to work together, to share ideas, to work towards goals common to the rest of the small group. And the teacher is freed to work among them giving help where she perceives its need to be.

But there are some problems with this classroom arrangement, too. It is clearly inappropriate for class discussion or for whole class activities like the sharing of a class novel or play. All the indications from the seating arrangements are that students should work in their small group almost to the exclusion of the other small groups; they face inwards and offer only their back views to their classmates.

A solution would be to move the furniture when a class activity was planned, but there is a need for frequent class discussion, at least every session, and the inevitable disruption that moving heavy tables about would cause is not acceptable because of the time it would take, the disruption it would cause and the noise it would create.

Another significant problem is that it is very difficult for students to form into different groupings. On coming into class, students will tend to go to the same seats and having got to them it is not easy, because of the amount of furniture and the lack of space in all but the biggest classrooms, for them to reorganise into new groups. Yet it is limiting to their learning experience for the same small group to work together for any length of time, whether it is a group of friends or a group composed by the teacher.

Model C

A solution to these difficulties might be found in the arrangement illustrated in Example C.

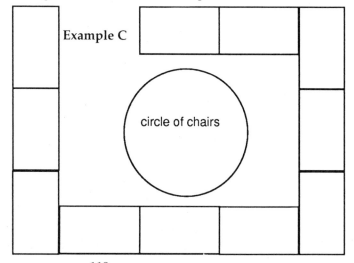

Example C

circle of chairs

In this arrangement the tables are up against the classroom walls and on them are the resources described earlier: the lesson ideas box, the resource material, dictionaries, art box and magazines box. On the walls are the displays, the class library, source books and reference books. Behind the screen is the computer terminal. The chairs form a circle in the middle of the classroom and when the students enter the room they sit along with the teacher facing inwards so that each can clearly see the front view of all of the others.

The first thing one notices in this arrangement is the amount of room there is: the tables are out of the way only to be brought into play when students need a surface on which to press; the chairs, free of tables, can easily be carried to the part of the room where they are needed or tucked under the tables to make space for a drama session. All this space makes it possible for the students to move easily about the room

- forming into groups;
- fetching whatever materials they need;
- conducting their research;
- keeping in touch with the work of others;
- presenting their finished products.

Despite the openly democratic arrangement of the chairs the behaviour of students is somehow constrained, perhaps by the exposure felt in the absence of the protective desk or the seclusion and complicity enjoyed by the back row gang. With all chairs being equal it is difficult, too, for students to feel any sense of territory: one part of the circle is much like any other, so it is harder to form recalcitrant knots or mischievous hierarchies.

More positively, it means that listening to a class text is far more natural when you can lift your eyes from the book to the face of the reader, and, being more natural, it is also easier to be involved and easier to concentrate. Since it is also more natural to hold a conversation on equal terms with people whose expression and gestures you can see and respond to, class discussions can be far more productive when held in this arrangement. And in neither example does the position of the teacher make her dominance of the activity inevitable. The sense of equality allied to the framework of formality provided by the circle can enable students to talk with more confidence and, consequently, at greater length.

Negotiation of the curriculum - when the teacher and students determine which activities individuals, groups or the whole class will next embark on - can also be entered into on more equal terms, with the result that students will be inclined to think more carefully about what they would like to do in their English time that would be beneficial as well as enjoyable for them.

Other Requirements
A Typical Lesson

More Student Choice

A typical session in the classroom model shown in Example C might be the reading of a short story followed by small group discussions which would necessitate movement out of the circle to strategic points about the room, then reporting back in the circle. Negotiation as to which activities would be carried out, followed by students singly, in pairs and in groups moving out of the circle to work on a range of options; then the sharing of the finished work and a period of evaluation and reflection, in other words:
• stimulus;
• response one: small group discussion;
• reporting back;
• negotiation;
• response two: choice of activity;
• sharing and evaluation.
are in this setting made more feasible, the stages more productive, because of the space which the students can enjoy.

An alternative way of working would be this: on the arrival of the students, who seat themselves in the circle, the teacher would ask which of them have work in progress and which have (English) work that they would like to begin. Following discussions on the merits of their proposals – the continuation of a private novel, the group writing of a quest story, the writing of a broadsheet on animal rights – various individuals and groups would break from the circle and begin their work. If no-one were using the computer or tape recording facilities the teacher might ask for a group of students to form and do some language work which would call this equipment into play. Left with perhaps half the class the teacher would then continue work on whatever comprised her syllabus, a module on Marilyn Monroe, for example, or work on 'description'.

The Small Room

Even in a very large room a screen is only a partial solution to the problem of distraction by noise or hectic movement, and there will undoubtedly be both if students are encouraged to use group discussion, role play and drama work regularly in their exploration of literature and their own language resources. Ideally, one wants a small room adjoining the classroom, with a tape recorder for the study or playing back of group discussions or simulations.

This proposal sounds idealistic to the point of irresponsibility but if, in fact, for small room you read office or large cupboard it becomes far less improbable. By a process of bartering and persuasion I managed to exchange a couple of flat cupboards with ample storage for a walk-in cupboard that would accommodate a small group, and a Year Head swopped offices to be nearer the administrative centre of the school, to our mutual benefit. But it could be that there is some nearby area of the school that is not much used that could become an extension to the English classroom and used by small groups for discussion or drama work. In any case, even if as a last resort all that can be found is a nearby stairwell, some space outside the classroom is very useful for those noisier activities that would disrupt the other students if held in the classroom.

All of which,
• the student choice;
• the resulting range of activities;
• drama or discussion work in a small room or stairwell close to the classroom;
pre-supposes a simple and foolproof system of monitoring, checking and reporting back that will hold even at the end of a long term when exhaustion is causing the most energetic teacher to flag. For the small room suggestion might only be the beginning of out-of-classroom work conducted by individuals and small groups:

122

•GCSE assignments, for example, make it increasingly necessary for students to travel to and from the library for information and for more lengthy research.

•Other English classrooms might be visited so that more expensive and therefore scarcer resources might be used or that work in the form of a play, a speech or some research findings might find a wider audience.

•Other parts of the school might be visited by groups of students filling out a questionnaire made up by themselves or investigating the possibility of, say, the removal of a mound at the edge of the playing fields or its conversion into a vivarium.

•Beyond the school grounds altogether work might be done into the status given to literature by the town, the way language is used in selling, or the written language environment of the town.

•Cross-curricular or cross-phase work might necessitate visits to the classrooms of other subjects or to neighbouring feeder schools.

A Suite of Rooms

In each school the solution to the problem of limited space will be different. The classroom layout illustrated in Example C has a persuasive degree of flexibility, but there is a need to look beyond the room itself, to an adjoining small space for taping, even to an additional space for drama work. A suite of English rooms would allow for a pooling of resources, copies of poems that work, the computer terminal, the video equipment and perhaps some reprographics machinery. It would give ready access to stores of books and other centralised material. It would facilitate team teaching and easy congress between teachers and students from other classes.

CHAPTER TWO

THE CLASS

A look at students' learning experiences in a setted and a mixed ability classroom. After concluding that there are more advantages for the student in a mixed ability class some suggestions are made with regard to organisational detail. Finally a detailed example of a teacher's scheme of work for a mixed ability Year 10 class is given. Just as the lack of one's own classroom would not make student-orientated teaching impossible, nor would working with a setted class. But both would undoubtedly make it more difficult ...

Setting
Some Assumptions Behind Setting

One assumption that lies behind the organisation of students into ability sets is that the teacher can teach didactically from the front of the class to the whole class, all of whose members would be at more or less the same stage in an aspect of their language development. To teach in this way would be more efficient because the teacher would not have to repeat herself to individuals and small groups but instead transmit her knowledge to all the students at the same time. Material would be chosen carefully so that there was a match between the ability of the class and the (intellectual) demands made by the text or the exercise.

Competition

Reinforcing this organisation might be a system of marks and examinations. High achievers might be rewarded within sets and slackers called to task. If any students exhibited consistent over- or underachievement, if the match or the pace proved inappropriate to them, they could be moved correspondingly up or down to a more suitable set.

The dynamic that energised this organisation would be one of interpersonal rivalry. The ideal would be to become upwardly mobile: part of the motive for work would be to outdo fellow classmates; the syllabus would be moved through as quickly as possible.

The scenario is a bracing one, of students striving to better themselves through strenuous competition by working with material chosen to extend and satisfy their intellectual and emotional demands - emotional too,

124

because of the assumed co-relation between students' cognitive and affective development.

Teachers might specialise so that one would work more with top sets on academic studies while another, with a gift for managing the more 'difficult' bottom sets, would spend much of her time with them.

Didactic Teaching

Sessions could be stimulating, even memorable, if the mode of delivery and the nature and complexity of the material did match the ability of the students. But if the teacher were going to be successful in this didactic role, as centre of attention and source of knowledge, she would need to have

• extensive experience of working with students of that particular ability;

• considerable specialist knowledge of the area under study so that students could be given detailed knowledge when they needed it;

• a wide-ranging and well-stocked mind enabling her to draw into her delivery issues of specific and general interest;

• an articulacy that makes listening to her and following her argument relatively easy, because she avoids unnecessary jargon of a subject-specific or a class/age kind and talks with fluency and animation;

• the ability to draw her students into class discussion by the posing of challenging questions of an open and conversational kind, and to listen attentively and responsively to what is said;

• some performance skills, being able to enliven a session with her own vibrant presence or enact the role of class animateur.

There is an important place in all English classrooms for vibrant, didactic teaching, for the charismatic, lively-minded, entertaining teacher who can enthuse a class with her own pleasure in and knowledge of literature, stimulate students to write with imagination and care, and help them enjoy the language. And there is a place for competition, particularly when it is directed inward rather than against classmates and more of a gentle inclination to improve than an anxiety.

Open Access

Sometimes a department will grade literature, matching it to the perceived ability of each set so that a range of short stories might be offered like this:

Set 1: *The Drowned Giant* - Gabriel García Márquez
Set 2: *Metamorphosis* - Franz Kafka
Set 3: *Occurence at Owl Creek Bridge* - Ambrose Bierce
Set 4: *The End of Something* - Ernest Hemingway
Set 5: *Beany* - Phillippa Pearce
Set 6: *The Lion* - Walter Macken
Set 7: *Seventeen Oranges* - Bill Naughton
Set 8: *The Ice Warrior* - Robin Chambers

All of these are good short stories that might be read by students across the Year 11 ability range, though some would require more time than others and the more complex would need imaginative handling by the teacher if weaker students particularly were not to be left bewildered.

But unless ways are found by the teacher to introduce all upper school students to a Shakespeare play, a challenging poem, a novel by a writer like Dickens, or Dhondy, or Darke, not all will enjoy the benefit of a study of literature that can thrill or amaze or open their eyes to the strange corners of our human experience, or to the full potential of language. If a school trip to a Shakespeare play or the study of *The Crucible* is only available to students in higher sets, a cultural apartheid tends to develop, based on preconceptions of the ability of those in lower sets who may not have been given a proper chance to reveal their potential. And their potential may not be shown nor their personalities thrive if their classroom experience is of didactic teaching only and of literature of limited scope.

The Nature of Literature

A text is worth studying if something about it is done well. It may be that the story is well-told, or the descriptions are evocative; perhaps it is very funny or diverting or a pleasure to read; perhaps the characters spring off the page, or the dialogue is realistic. Perhaps it is disturbing, or puzzling, or illuminating, or unaccountably memorable.

More often than not a text will work on many levels: it will be worth reading for the story, to find out what happens, and it will contain convincing characters and vividly drawn descriptions. There will be particular scenes and climaxes that stand out; there will be atmosphere and mood, perhaps a web of imagery that runs through the text unifying it and conveying a resonance on a personal and impersonal level. So the reader can respond intellectually, imaginatively, emotionally, aesthetically or spiritually to the text and the best readers will respond in all these ways. A play like *Macbeth* or a novel like *Great Expectations* will be accessible, on one level or another or on several levels, to pretty well all the students in Year 11, and it is not the limitation of the students but the nature of the delivery and the morale of the class that will determine how successful such an encounter will be.

Teachers' Expectations

The Californian research which investigated the effect on students' performance of teachers' expectations is well-known. The students involved were all of the same ability but, as one would expect, the teachers who had been told that they had classes of very bright students found that their results were better than those achieved by their colleagues who had been told that their students were weak. The more surprising research was that done with rats, all of which were untrained. Scientists were told that one batch of rats was trained and the other wild and in their reports duly described much better responses, even far fewer bites, from the former than from the latter group! The not-so-hidden curriculum for the teachers of lower set students tells them that they should not expect a high standard from their charges because of their limited ability. Consequently the material used can be less demanding and less rewarding and the assignments of a low level: because some teachers don't expect a high standard anyway, the students' performance can be predictably poor. So the cycle of low achievement and low expectation continues.

Students' Morale

If the student perceives that he is weak at a subject, it is likely he will not commit himself seriously to it and he will fail. Having gained no satisfaction at all from one activity, merely a confirmation that he cannot perform adequately with his own language or enjoy working with it, he will be even less inclined to work with care and at length the next time. When a whole set of 'low ability' students is formed this can be the experience of every member. Morale is destined to remain at a very low ebb so that disillusionment and cynicism can set in, finding expression in indiscipline and unruliness.

Classroom Ambience

And when there is noise or the threat of indiscipline the conditions necessary for learning do not exist. It is not possible for any of the students to work hard for any significant length of time. Thoughtful spoken or written composition cannot occur in an atmosphere of rowdiness or under the threat of mockery. Assignments that are completed with perfunctoriness deny the opportunity for improvement. It is not uncommon for the standard of attainment of students in bottom sets actually to decline in the upper school years.

Discipline

In such circumstances the teacher can be driven to be disciplinarian, to hold the fort from the front, and, if necessary, to shout and to threaten. How else can she punish but by setting more work or by keeping students in, both of which will only further alienate students who might have little enough liking for the subject or the school environment as it is. Often lower set classes are made up not only of students who do have significant intellectual limitations but also of students who under-achieve because they lack motivation. It is in the nature of setting that students will remain with more or less the same classmates up through the school, which can mean that by the time a lower set reaches Year 10 or 11 the shared resentment against the establishment presents an insuperable barrier to real learning.

Increasing Disparity Between Sets

As the sets proceed up through the school, so the experiences of those students in higher and lower sets diverge more and more. Those in the higher sets will tend daily to experience orderliness, tentative, speculative discourse, richly imagined and highly wrought literature, a sense of recognised achievement and a growing sense of self-respect; while their peers in the lower sets may have a

128

daily fare of cultural and social disorder. While the one is enjoying the civilising influence of views being thoughtfully expressed and received, of literature being read in calm and tolerant circumstances, of the pleasures and fun in learning, the other might be absorbing the principles of misrule: cynicism and intolerance. Students who enter school with the same potential for learning might leave with attitudes to life and aspirations that are far apart.

Mixed Ability Classes
Students' Needs

If the image of teacher as transmitter of knowledge lies behind the setting approach to class organisation it is teacher as facilitator that informs the mixed ability model. Sometimes teachers will work with a mixed ability class from the front in a didactic or inspirational mode, but there is a danger that no student will learn satisfactorily if the teacher works routinely in this way and does not cater for the skills and abilities of the individuals that make up the class.

More often the teacher will work alongside the student, talking over a piece of work, moving him on, encouraging him all the time to recognise that it is he who has the responsibility for his learning. She, the teacher, will do all she can to facilitate the learning, providing direction, suggestions, resources, equipment and the background organisation necessary for a range of activities to take place, but it is he who must do it, do the thinking, the problem-solving, the creating, the crafting, the analysing. No-one but he can do those things that in the end are going to bring about learning and give satisfaction. And to be a successful learner he needs to be encouraged to feel that

- he has experiences, stories, points of view and insights that are of interest to the other members of the class;
- he has the means of expressing them;
- he has the opportunity to express them in a variety of contexts;
- he will be listened to and his views respected, by his teacher and his classmates;
- he will be able to work individually, in pairs, in small groups and as part of a whole class;
- he will have the opportunity to succeed in a variety of

activities;

- he is able to share his work routinely with the other members of the class;
- his teacher will enable him to feel secure when he takes risks in his work;
- no limits will be set to the nature of language work he can attempt or the quality of work he might produce;
- he can attempt a variety of activities, none of which is seen as superior to another;
- his teacher and his classmates will work collaboratively with him so that together progress can be made;
- he will be expected to work hard, but he will determine the pace at which he works and progresses;
- he will have access to the same learning experiences as his classmates, if he is responsible enough to take advantage of them;
- to some extent he will be able to influence his curriculum.

And the successful mixed ability English teacher would need to

- feel a close affinity for all her students and a respect for their needs, social and academic;
- take pleasure in the slightest achievement of the least as well as the most able;
- believe that her students should be enabled to become independent as well as collaborative learners;
- be able to judge when to intervene in individual and group activities with a sureness and delicacy of touch that can only come from working closely with students over time;
- be able to support students by asking the right questions or offering the appropriate avenue for thought or action;
- be able to draw on a great deal of assimilated knowledge about the language and language development whenever necessary;
- be able to sense the time for a change of material, mood or activity;
- be able to organise herself, her room, her resources and her students so that muddles are by and large avoided;
- be able to draw on an infinite source of energy and inspiration!

There are very few comprehensive schools that have

mixed ability organisation in every subject, so students often come to English with a perception of their comparative ability formed by the sets they are in elsewhere in the school; but once a mixed ability English class has established a high morale for itself, and it will do if the above conditions can be met, there is the chance for those students who come with a sense of inadequacy to start to believe in themselves as potentially successful learners.

Staff Morale

The morale of students depends to a large extent on the morale of teachers, which is likely to be higher if they are working for a department organising its students into mixed ability classes. The reasons for this are as follows:
• There will be no reason for partisan interests, grievances or misunderstandings to develop if teachers are all involved in the same work.
• Teachers will have similar classroom experiences and they will be able to share them informally in the staffroom and formally at department meetings.
• They will be able to plan together to develop a curriculum in which they are all involved.
• They can work together to produce resources that can be pooled and shared by the whole department.
• They will all have the same purpose, the same problems to overcome and the same targets to aim for.
• A success in one classroom can have repercussions for the practice in all the others.

Such teacher interaction can lead to a very sophisticated appreciation of teaching practice and the learning process.

Planning Details
The Headteacher and Governors

The Headteacher and governors would have to be convinced that planning and preparation for a change to mixed ability organisation had been thorough. This would not involve the mass production of worksheets, a phenomenon that held up the development of good mixed ability teaching in the past, but
• a serious study of teaching and learning styles;
• careful preparation of schemes of work;
• the observation and analysis of good classroom practice;
• a programme of talks to the department by local teachers

who work successfully with mixed ability classes and would not mind their arguments being thoroughly analysed;

• the study of books and articles on the subject by former teachers like Richard Mills, Mike Torbe and David Jackson;

• the production of a paper outlining the philosophy and the intended practice, for the Head's perusal and for possible dissemination.

The Deputy Headteacher

It might mean that the Deputy Headteacher would have to make certain adjustments to the timetable. If English were blocked against Mathematics or Science, in which the students were setted, it would not be possible to organise mixed ability classes in English. English would either have to be blocked on its own, which would require a large number of specialist English teachers all available at the same time, or blocked against a subject or group of subjects taken by all the students whose teachers were happy to work with mixed ability classes.

The Parents

A broadsheet going to every home advising parents of any intended shift in teaching style would give the basic information, but much more direct would be a meeting or two at the school at which parents could listen to the case being put by the Head of Department and members of the department who might talk to the previously circulated broadsheet.

After a short plenary, parents could accompany the teacher of their own children to her classroom where she might demonstrate a typical mixed ability session so that parents could experience for themselves what English might be like for their children. A question and answer session might follow, using the material of the specimen lesson as a basis for discussion, and in such a small forum the atmosphere could be informal and genuinely informative. The evening could be rounded off by all parents and English teachers gathering again in the hall to meet over coffee or a glass of wine.

Class Organisation

Since GCSE is a two-year course it is best for a class to stay together and keep the same teacher throughout Years

10 and 11. At the end of Years 7, 8 and 9 though, it may be beneficial for classes to be reconstituted and, at the same time, for all students to be given a different English teacher. Much of the work in the English classroom depends on talk, the exchange of experiences and the collaborative development of understanding, and each student can gain social, intellectual and linguistic benefit from interaction with the other members of the class. But after a year of working together collaboration could become rather routine and predictable: to create new classes of students annually might keep alive the sense of freshness and discovery.

The best way of achieving this reconstitution of classes is by making use of a record of achievement like the one described in Chapter Seven, which is integral to the education process and involves the student throughout in his self-evaluation.

Working through these records and checking through the students' files the department, working together, could reorganise the students into new classes for the coming year, making sure that each class had in it students who were keen to talk in different situations and with a wide range of ability, interests and motivation. Those who had had a negative influence on each other would be separated by being placed in different classes.

Support Teachers

When a department goes fully mixed ability and the students who had previously been withdrawn are also incorporated into the new classes, the former special needs teachers will now be able to work in the mainstream. They might become a peripatetic support service, moving from class to class as they are needed. Their role might be
• to work alongside students in the act of composition;
• to supervise groups doing drama or having a discussion;
• to accompany students to the library or on activities beyond the school grounds;
• to visit homes of students with particular difficulties;
• to monitor the progress of students giving cause for concern.

Some departments offer occasional short options programmes in which a number of modular courses are

133

presented and students sign up for the one they wish to take. The support teachers in such circumstances might offer courses along with the other English teachers.

The Department Scheme of Work

Every school has a development plan, a response to the National Curriculum and to the LEA curriculum policy document. This plan states the school aims and objectives and the means by which they will be delivered throughout the school. The aims will be worthy, unexceptional statements, like
•to help students to develop lively, enquiring minds, the ability to question and argue rationally and to apply themselves to tasks and physical skills;
•to develop in students a sense of self-respect, the capacity to live as independent, self-motivated adults, and the ability to function collaboratively in society.

The schemes of work for each department have to reflect these broad aims as well as the subject-specific programmes of study as laid down by the National Curriculum, and show in some detail how both will be experienced by the students.

The department scheme of work, then, should ensure that the students have a broad, balanced and differentiated curriculum, that there is a coherence to the work of the department and that the department needs in terms of teachers, time, rooms and resources have been clearly identified. It will provide the philosophical and practical basis for the work of the department, and as such should have been produced in the first place by all members of the department working together; and it should be seen as a document undergoing continual revision.

It is impossible to be definitive about how a department scheme of work should be structured but the main headings could be:
•Title
•Aims
•Objectives
•General Policy
•Learning Strategies
•Progression
•Programmes of Study

- Resources
- Learning Objectives
- Classroom Organisation
- Assessment
- Evaluation.

**General Department
Policies**

The first six headings represent the general policies of the department, and it is here that statements on such issues as the organisation of students to setted or mixed ability classes might appear. If a department were to consider a change of organisation from, say, setting to mixed ability, it would have to go about it with caution. Because the aims of the school are presented in such broad terms it is unlikely that they would of themselves stop a department from considering a different arrangement. But any radical departure from school practice, even if it were not stated policy, would have to be planned and carried out from the beginning with the full co-operation of the Headteacher and the governing body.

On page 137 is an example of a front-page format of an English teacher's scheme of work. It is designed to give a clear outline of the work that is to be covered, to focus on specific aspects of that work and as a reminder of some basic tenets. All teachers in the department would use the same format. They would probably have worked together on its design, making sure it was a match for the department scheme of work and accorded with the philosophy of the department, and that it was flexible enough to allow for individual teachers' approaches and for students to develop their own curricula if they so wished.

The top row of boxes is self-explanatory: the first would contain the subject of the programme of work - *Lord of the Flies*, a video of *Charlotte Dymond*, Dialogue, Growth, Ways of Telling Stories, Onomatopoeia - then which year group, for how long the unit would run and if there were to be any cross-curricular links (and if so, with whom). Department aims would be large, general statements, like 'to develop a love of literature in all the students' or 'to encourage students to become

135

independent learners'. In Main Purpose the teacher would list the objectives behind her work. These might be 'to study the way comedy works' or 'to explore how language is used to promote a particular point of view'. There might be a predominant 'language and learning' objective stated here too, like 'to encourage active listening skills' or 'to develop peer tutoring'.

In the column headed Activity the teacher would write the main sections of work - descriptive writing, a study of Frances Horovitz's *Country Afternoon*, simulation of a road accident - followed in the next by details of the process to be undergone (research, note-taking, interviewing), with whom it would be done (teacher, visiting speaker, students in pairs) and then the purpose behind the activity, the audience for whom it was intended and the proposed means of presentation.

There is no mention in this scheme of work of individual skills or statements of attainment because it is in the nature of English that a range of skills across the attainment targets and levels will be generated by almost every creative English session. What is more, the system of classroom organisation described in this section of the book ensures that the range is widened through routine processes of negotiation, collaboration, presentation and evaluation. It is in this context of challenging and purposeful activities that opportunities for the exercise and extension of skills occur.

Although the department scheme of work has to include the National Curriculum programmes of study which cover all the statements of attainment, it might be useful to keep a check on which particular statements of attainment are being generated by a teacher's planned activities. A column on individual students' needs might be useful as a prompt to take appropriate action. Because in English skills tend to be worked on in one to one situations while work is in progress and the occasion is right, a column has not been drawn in for them.

At the foot of the title page is a box for activities that would take place outside the classroom, the purpose of this being to remind the teacher about exit slips for library visits and arrangements for students leaving the school premises. Below is a box for resource requirements, and

136

alongside it one for assessment procedures and one for the means by which the whole unit of work will be evaluated.

TITLE OF WORK:	YEAR:	DURATION:	CROSS-CURRICULAR LINKS:

DEPARTMENT AIMS:

MAIN PURPOSE: (TEACHER'S)

ACTIVITY:	LEARNING PROCESS: (COLLABORATORS)	PURPOSE: (PUPIL'S)	AUDIENCE:	PRESENTATION:

OUT OF CLASSROOM:	ASSESSMENT:	EVALUATION:
RESOURCES:		

Overleaf is the title page of a teacher's scheme of work filled in with details of a unit based on the study of a short story called *Occurrence at Owl Creek Bridge*, written by Ambrose Bierce. It is followed up by specific activities of the type that would commonly be set up in the treatment of such a text.

TITLE OF WORK: An occurrence at Owl Creek Bridge	YEAR: 10	DURATION: ½ term	CROSS-CURRICULAR LINKS: Art department

DEPARTMENT AIMS: To foster a love of literature in the students
To foster in each student a respect for the abilities of his classmates

MAIN PURPOSE:
(TEACHER'S)
To study the short story form
To study descriptive writing by writing and reading
To focus on the narrative structure

ACTIVITY:	LEARNING PROCESS: (COLLABORATORS)	PURPOSE: (PUPIL'S)	AUDIENCE:	PRESENTATION:
A. Introductory descriptive exercises	Choice Writing/drafting All students to choose at least 3, working individually	Establish context Play with words Explore description, readers' needs Wall display	teacher peers class	Wall display
B. Background work into story's context	Research work in library Groups 2-6 Choice Reports to be written up	Inform rest of class on aspect of story's background	rest of class	to class, perhaps to rest of year
C. Read story	(prepare reading thoroughly)	Listening skills Pleasure in story	whole class	—
D. Response ① Retelling	Choice of written work drama discussion (group) interviews	Gain insight by writing & sharing creative responses	class	acting out before the class for evaluation
E. Response ② Written work	Discussion in groups then choice of titles and work in pairs	Finished essay	partner/ teacher	wall display
F. Film	Note-taking/discussion	Compare media	class	—
G. Reflection	Sharing/evaluating	make learning explicit	class	—
H. Follow-up	Individual choice Personal study	Independent learning Extend knowledge	self/ wide readership	sharing with rest of class

OUT OF CLASSROOM:
Library work/central library
Outside location for description
Art room

RESOURCES:
Owl Creek Bridge (30)
Ode to a Tomato (30)
Thistles (30)
Odour of chrysanthemums cloze (30)
Alice in Wonderland (5)
Gulliver's Travels (5)
Lost Love (5)

tape recorder
film projector
OHP

ASSESSMENT:
Ongoing throughout unit of oral and written work

Marking of written work mainly alongside the student in the classroom

EVALUATION:
Based on involvement of the students at various stages of unit and the quality of work also on their verbal feedback in the reflection session.

A: Introductory Descriptive Exercises

A sequence of sessions led by the teacher on descriptive writing. Students to work in pairs throughout in the polishing of their writing.

1. Make up your own words for ten sounds created by the teacher then choose the most appropriate English word; compare your coinages with the English words you have chosen. Study Ted Hughes's *Thistles* for onomatopoeia. Then write your own poem.

2. Write a poem about your stone after a class discussion based on description of the stones each student has brought in.

3. Read the poem *Ode to a Tomato* by Pablo Neruda and discuss. Eat slowly and carefully the fruit or vegetable you have brought to the classroom, then write your own poem in the style of Neruda's poem.

4. Compare the beginnings of several short stories: how do the authors interest the reader?

5. Make a cloze exercise of the first page of D. H. Lawrence's *Odour of Chrysanthemums*.

6. Study *Lost Love* by Robert Graves, and write your own version.

A series of exercises on description presented briefly by the teacher, from which each student does three. The students should work with at least one classmate to focus on the effectiveness of his descriptions. The finished work should be made into a display arranged by a student.

7. Describe either your
   pantry;
   loft;
   garden shed;
   bedroom;
   understairs;
   garage;
using three senses.

8. Describe a place well-known to you, using three senses.

9. Read the passage describing Crooks's room from *Of Mice and Men*, then describe the interior of a shop you know well, using one sense.

10. Describe a place you know well, in summer and in winter.

11. Describe an ordinary activity from the point of view of

139

Alice or Gulliver, very big and very small.
12. Describe the face of someone you know, as a young and as an old person.
13. Imagine yourself as an old person and describe your own hands.
14. Using a telescope, describe a scene from a hundred metres/twenty metres/one metre.
15. Describe a spider for a biology textbook/an encyclopaedia/a poem/a scene in a story.
16. Describe the school art room from your own careful observation.
17. Describe a scene through
    coloured glass;
    or smoke;
    or water;
    or foliage;
    or in sleep;
    or in the night;
    or in early morning mist.
18. Write a poem whose lines each begin 'Noses are ... '
19. Write a poem each line of which begins 'What I like about ... '
20. Play blindfold games/directions/guess the object.

B: Background Research Work

Students will work in groups (two-six), sometimes in the school library, sometimes in the central library. They should choose one of the subjects below, or one of their own choice, and prepare a report which they will give, using visual aids, to the class. One or two people might need to work in the art room.
   1. American Civil War
   2. Famous Paintings of the Civil War
   3. Capital Punishment
   4. Imprisonment
   5. The Ballad
   6. Paintings of War by Salvador Dali or Goya
   7. Music of War by Britten or Prokofiev
   8. Photography of War
   9. Espionage
   10. Pacifism

C: Read the Story

Next comes the reading of the short story. The teacher

140

might decide to read it herself if she can read aloud well, or she might prefer to ask individual students to prepare passages for homework which they would then read to the class. All the students would be issued with copies so that they could work on the story on their own.

D: Response through Retelling

The first response activity could be of a retelling or empathetic kind and might involve some of the following ideas. Students should work in groups of the appropriate size, probably pairs for the written and interview work and larger groups for the drama and discussion work. They should report their insights back to the class.

Group Written Work
1. The report of the spy
2. A different end
3. The diary of the wife
4. The officer's diary
5. The officer's report
6. Official letters
7. Newspaper accounts
8. War propaganda
9. Ballad writing
10. The diary of the spy

Group Drama Work
1. The scene with the spy
2. The arrest
3. The incident from the bridge
4. Home
5. The confession
6. The trial
7. The wife tells her grandchildren
8. The spy tells his colleagues
9. A rifleman tells his wife
10. Strange meeting - after death, meeting between spy and hanged man

Group Discussion Work
1. Why he tried to blow up the bridge
2. If he had escaped
3. Claustrophobia

4. Views on the part played by the spy
5. How would you illustrate/film this story? Plan in detail.

Interviews
1. With the army officer: how does he feel?
2. With the spy: how does he feel?
3. With the wife
4. With Ambrose Bierce: what was he trying to say? Was he pleased with his story?
5. With one of the riflemen who was on the bridge

E: Response through Written Work

After this work has been shared by the class the second response might be made, and now that the story has had time to sink in, this could take the form of a much closer look at the text. After a brief period of small group discussion based on the following leads, each student should choose one or an adaptation of one and write up a properly organised essay.
1. What clues are there in this story warning the reader what the ending will be?
2. What is the structure of the story?
3. Who tells the story?
4. How good are the beginning and end?
5. How do different parts of the story make you feel?
6. Who do you sympathise with?
7. What made you feel as you did?
8. Were you convinced by the story?
10. What does the story tell you about the Civil War?
11. What is the writer getting across to you about the Civil War or war in general?
12. What sort of writer is Ambrose Bierce?
13. What sort of man do you think is Ambrose Bierce?
14. Do you like this short story?
15. Is it a good short story?
16. Compare *Occurrence at Owl Creek Bridge* with other short stories you have read.

F: Film

The film of the short story should now be shown, the students taking notes for use in the susequent class discussion comparing the film with the short story.

G: Reflection

If there are any pieces of work that might usefully be shared with the class but have not yet been, this is the time. After that the students should have the opportunity first to discuss in full what has been learnt over this unit of work and then how useful and worthwhile they have found the experience.

H: Follow-up

At this point the teacher may wish to continue work on the same theme or enable certain (or all) of the students to select an area, like those below, for further study.
1. The Short Story
2. The Ballad
3. Westerns
4. The Hero
5. Carlos Fuentes's book *Old Gringo*, a fictional account of Ambrose Bierce, who disappeared mysteriously into South America
6. Ambrose Bierce, journalist

Rich Language Experience

It should be a strength of the mixed ability class that there is a great variety of experience on offer, with class members from backgrounds across the social spectrum and distinctive ways of expressing themselves. This range of experience and expression should create a rich fund of stories, attitudes, perceptions and ways of saying things to broaden the perspectives of each one. In a constructive and energetic ambience in which students are engaged in purposeful listening and talking they should find that their appreciation of 'the use of language' and their own ability to use it will steadily develop.

CHAPTER THREE

FULL CLASS ACTIVITIES

Now a description of full class activities, beginning with the class reader and going on to the thematic approach and extended simulations. In each section the urge to tell stories reveals itself. Not only are we drawn strongly towards the stories of others, but we also seem to have a facility for telling our own stories and a need to exercise that facility.

The Class Reader
Personal Growth

The English teacher's subject for study is 'the use of language'. Language is all about making meaning, and so it is the issue of what the other person is saying, how she is saying it and how we in turn might make our meanings that is our major concern. And it is because language is so close to ourselves, because we are to a large extent defined as individuals by our use of language, how much and in what circumstances we use it, what phraseology we employ, how we articulate it, what we choose to use it for, that the study of 'the use of language' becomes, to some extent, a study of human behaviour. Argument is 'a primary act of mind' as is storytelling, so that much of our study of 'the use of language' would be occupied with the response to and the composition of these two modes of expression. And because neither of these modes works only on the intellectual level, but very much on the emotional, the aesthetic, spiritual and moral, we find that the 'use of language' curriculum harmonises with the 'personal growth' curriculum that is in the mainstream of all conscientious English teaching.

The Importance of Story

One of our main means of attempting to make sense of ourselves and the world of people and things around us is by telling stories. We tell them to divert, to amuse, to escape, and for pleasure in the words, in the composition, in the humour. And we tell them, and this is where the deeper motivation for storytelling might lie, to express some mystery, in the hope that the retelling or the response might shed some light.

Cycling to school one day, on my first job, I came across two blackbirds that had just been hit by a car. Beside the road watching these two birds, fatally injured,

144

fluttering about in front of them, were two workmen in a galvanised hut having their breakfast. I stopped and killed the two birds to put them out of their misery and, thoroughly miserable, remounted and rode on while the workmen, still munching, watched the proceedings. At school I told various people about this incident, teachers and students, and in time I tried to organise it into a poem. To me it was one of those things that you cannot forget or ever really come to terms with. So you keep mulling it over and bringing it up as I have here.

And having done this, and indulged myself, such is the delight in and the impetus for storytelling that half a dozen more stories have come to mind, some less narrative than image like that of my grandmother, at that time a woman of ninety-four, standing at the grave of her brother after the funeral party had dispersed, silent and still, for what seemed like five minutes, before being led away by her son.

These incidents, along with snatches of literature, other people's stories, provide me with a kind of personal history that puts a context around whatever significant happens now.

Much is claimed for literature and there is no doubt that sometimes it is good to go to a favourite book for stimulus or soothing. My grandfather went to *Pilgrim's Progress*. I like to read Patrick White's *Tree of Man*. They become part of our personal baggage. As English teachers, if we want our students to enjoy the benefits of well-told stories and introduce them to some of the stories that will become part of the backcloth to their lives, we need to provide them with a wealth of novels, plays and poems. There should be the opportunity for reading and moving on, for careful analysis of the subject matter and at times a close scrutiny of the style, the narrative treatment, the techniques of characterisation and description, the use of language.

The Style

So we arrive at style. As well as a study of the behaviour of the characters and thematic issues, the students should consider how the author achieved her effects:

• How was the language used to catch your attention as a

145

reader?
- How was the atmosphere created?
- How was this character so vividly drawn?
- Who tells the story?
- What was it about the use of language that made you feel quite like that?
- How is the story organised?
- What gives this book its identity?
- What has been put in? What left out?

If English is about the 'use of language', then literature must be at the heart of the curriculum and literature seen as artefact, something created out of words by someone with something to communicate. Part of our job as teachers should be, then, to give students the chance to respond to such work and, to deepen that response, to study how it was made.

Some Problems with Class Readers

Class readers seem like an efficient means of introducing books to students and of encouraging thoughtful consideration of social, linguistic and literary issues. But it is difficult to manage the class reader approach satisfactorily. My daughter came back from school the other day with her new class reader, Judy Blume's *Tiger Eyes*: she settled down that night and read the whole of it. This would have been fine if her teacher had developed a system of class management enabling her to talk over this book in a group, do some written work on it for her file and move on to something else. But sadly she was destined to spend the next month in her English sessions listening to the story being read round the class with features discussed intermittently, until she became very bored.

Reading a novel so slowly with so many interruptions goes against the natural impulses of the keen reader who wants more than anything to find out what happens. His need to know the outcome is being constantly frustrated by what Michael Benton calls the 'pantechnicon' approach, in which the teacher chugs along a predetermined route of assignments, a character study, a piece of descriptive writing, an essay exploring one of the major themes of the book thus far. He mustn't be allowed to read on or he will have covered the ground before the rest of the class arrives and, what is more, he might reveal the end, spoiling the rest of the reading for his classmates as well. So another natural impulse, to share with others through dramatic retelling the favourite and most affecting bits of the story, has also to be denied him.

To punctuate a class reader with frequent pauses for the clarification of difficult passages is also a hindrance to the students. If the book is gripping they will not want to dwell on small details and lose the sense of atmosphere and tension that is so important to their enjoyment of the book.

Alternatives

There are, though, ways round these problems:
• The novel chosen does not have to be of the length of *The Grapes of Wrath* or *Great Expectations*. Novellas like D. H. Lawrence's *The Fox* or *The Virgin and the Gypsy*, John Steinbeck's *Of Mice and Men*, Alex La Guma's *A Walk in the Night*, George Orwell's *Animal Farm* or Janni Howker's *Isaac Campion* can be read in a little over a week in the usual time allocated to English in the upper school if read straight through to the class by the teacher.
• Even a full length book will last no more than two and a half weeks if it is read with no pause during lesson time. There is no need to keep stopping for clarification: if the book has been well chosen, the general sense will be clear and further elucidation can be done to better effect once the text is partially known.
• Some written work can be carried out alongside the text for homework, especially work of an empathetic nature – the keeping of a diary of one of the characters, for example, or a reading log.
• The occasional, well-timed pause for a class discussion or a piece of writing or drama predicting the next stage of the story can enhance the story and increase students' involvement. Natural responses to a story, like empathising, reflecting, predicting, analogising and evaluating can be made, to personalise and enrich the reading experience.
• A film of the book can be shown so that students can compare their interpretation of the text to that of the film director.
• The occasional cloze or Bob Moy's Tray microcomputer

exercise, designed to reveal through students' small group discussion the author's particular style, can be used. (In the preparation of the cloze passages the teacher might take out all the verbs or all the images, offering four alternatives for each gap.)

•Students who have already read the text intended as the class reader, or who wish to read on at home and will therefore soon go ahead of the rest of the class, might be allowed to do their own work.

•If *The Old Man and the Sea*, say, has been read by some students who do not wish to get further into the novella by a re-reading they might either read another book by Hemingway or a book on the same theme.

•Similarly the quicker reader might wish to supplement the main class reader with a second book or some associated literature or do more assignments based on the class text. The teacher's main intention has still been served, that all members of the class have read a demanding and worthwhile book on which a variety of work can be set and shared.

•And if it becomes clear midway through a novel that the students are bored and no amount of dramatised reading, explanation or cajoling will take them to the end, it should be abandoned. Some might wish to finish it but as an experience for the whole class it would only be negative.

The Teacher's Choice

Class readers should be a challenging read on one level or another: they would have to be well-crafted books with a substantial plot, subtle and convincing characterisation and an imaginatively realised theme. They should have 'changed the author ' in their writing and have the potential to 'change their readers' too.

The chosen text might be a book that past experience had shown to be a success with other upper school students, one that students of this age were known – perhaps through their review writing – to have enjoyed, or one that the teacher had read and was convinced would be suitable.

Some heads of department buy small sets of six and if they prove popular among the students build them up to class set size.

Ownership

The teacher has to like the book too, but not possessively. Marjorie Hourd wrote that you should never select literature for use with children that you do not yourself value highly; you should not, though, be possessive of it but hand it over to them. If they take it and warm to it, well and good. But if they reject it or for some reason do not respond favourably to it, the teacher should not take this personally: it is now theirs.

I have taught *The Old Man and the Sea* several times, loving every moment of it, reading to the end choking with emotion, giving the last three pages to some stony-hearted student to read when I felt I could croak out no more. But no class of mine has ever enjoyed it. A good teacher would have dropped it from her repertoire and accepted that it was a bad choice, but I persisted and continued to fail with it. Yet I still have the feeling, as with another failure of mine, Alan Garner's *Stone Book*, that given the right context and presentation it would be a success.

A Balance

Without going all the way with David Holbrook, who believes that literature used in the classroom should be 'life-enhancing', it is certainly true that many texts selected as class readers are very bleak. When the upper school fare is *Z for Zachariah*, *Children of the Dust*, *Lord of the Flies*, *Brothers in the Land* and Ian Sharp's play *The Genesis Roadshow*, it is surprising that Year 11 students can get themselves out of bed in the morning to face life again.

If the teacher is going to assume control of students' reading to the extent that she may do where class readers are the norm, a balance ought to be struck. There is no reason why Robert Cormier's *Bumblebees Fly Any How* should not be used as long as it can be fully discussed, but such a hard-hitting novel should find its place in the context of other literature which presents life in more cheerful circumstances. *Bumblebees Fly Any How* is 'life-enhancing' but it is so chilling and disturbing that a teacher would probably wish to lighten the mood by following it with a text easier on the emotions.

Sharing a Class Novel

Yet, despite these provisos, there are many things to be

149

said in favour of this common classroom activity:
- A class of students has been taken together, sometimes sleepily and grudgingly but at times most enthusiastically, through a worthwhile novel.
- A wide range of good literature can be introduced.
- Because the book has been read in class you have ensured that all members of the class in attendance have heard the whole of it; and it is extremely doubtful whether, without this approach, some students would read a novel at all.
- This shared experience can be used to good effect in group and class discussion and in a range of optional activities. In this way individuals can make of the text what they can by using their abilities in drama, art work and through writing to create a variety of responses.
- When these responses are brought together by the teacher to be shared by the whole class all members will gain from the insights and efforts of each individual.

Epistemic Comprehension

Iser is the educationalist responsible for the reappraisal of how literature can be best handled in the classroom. His work has much influenced the thinking of Michael and Peter Benton, and of Gordon Wells, who calls the creative retelling of a story 'epistemic' comprehension. By this he means a retelling that grows up between the text and the individual, so that the experience and personality of the reader react with the text and a new meaning is embodied in a new piece of writing or some other artefact. Wells shows a videotape of a Canadian primary school class discussing *The Ballad of Yukon Jake* in small groups with very little intervention by the teacher, certainly no answers being provided, and making three-dimensional constructions and other creations in response to the poem. This sort of approach enables a shared experience to develop along whatever lines the individuals in the class care to take it: as a creative response it explores the work under study to a considerable, and personal, depth.

A Standpoint

But the student's active reading should not be left there. It is important, too, that he thinks himself round the book to ask
- Why it might have become a class reader;

150

- Out of what environment and what social context the book grew;
- What is the author's particular standpoint?
- What are the particular techniques she uses to present her case?
- Who are her publishers?
- What would happen to the reader's response to the lead characters if instead of being white they were black, instead of being female they were male, instead of being native they were foreign; if instead of being set in England the book were set in Spain or South Africa?
- What if, instead of one thing happening, the author had decided that something else would happen?

Selective Reading

In a mixed ability class particularly, not all of a full-length novel would necessarily be read by all the students. Significant passages might be read by the teacher or students who have been asked to prepare a reading, parts read at home and related by students with the backup of the teacher, parts narrated by the teacher. Parts might be acted out, either as a means of gaining deeper understanding of what has been read by the actual physical involvement of the students and the intellectual energy released by the creative act of dramatisation, or of assimilating the implications of the scene by using drama to develop the story in whatever direction the students' imagination takes it. By this means another plot is brought into being, co-existing alongside the original which it will illuminate through comparison and challenge.

Other Strategies

In schools where students would not read on their own, one class novel a year seems appropriate, though if the teacher is particularly good at reading prose aloud with the skill to bring a story vividly alive for her students, it would be a pity not to use this approach more frequently.

Apart from class readers, however, there are other strategies that might be used to encourage students to read more fiction:
- The teacher who is encouraging individual reading might ask students when they complete a private reader to tell the class about it, describing their reactions and

151

giving reasons for their opinion of it.

•The beginnings of various novels or character studies, episodes or descriptions might be selected for comparison and discussion.

•Extracts might be looked at which illustrate a particular stylistic feature. In this way the teacher might encourage students, if a passage appeals to them, to read the whole novel themselves.

•Writers might be invited into the school.

•Students might be invited to write to an author.

•They might be asked to role-play a writer, or the editor interviewing a writer.

•Time might be given in class for private reading of books chosen by the students individually.

•Films and videos of books might be used.

•Students might be encouraged to publish their own novels to complement the class library.

•It might be acknowledged that we choose a book depending on our state of mind, somebody's recommendation or the amount of time we have, or by how long it is, what the printing is like or the picture on the cover; and that to be able to choose is as necessary to our students as it is to us.

Short Stories and Poems

As far as the class study of literature is concerned, since the study of class novels is problematic, some teachers rely instead on short stories and poetry. A short story can be read, usually, in a single period and the impact can be immediate. The techniques of writing can be easily discussed, and for class discussion purposes, because of the brevity of short stories and poems, they are most suitable for close reference and comparison. An open class discussion I recall comparing Leon Garfield's *Strange Fish* and Phillippa Pearce's *Beany* convinces me that, however one might make a case for small group work, full class open discussion can develop a co-operative energy and coherence peculiarly its own.

The Thematic Approach

When I first began teaching I planned a developmental curriculum starting in Year 7 with lessons based on the significance behind single words: nicknames, pets' names, place names, opposites; each topic giving rise to class discussions, study of extracts and some personal writing. I moved on up through the school looking at story-telling in genres – fairy story, fable, myth, and on to westerns, science fiction, detective stories and romances. I looked at story-telling techniques like how the plot was delivered, structured, revealed; then I moved on to characterisation. The students could focus on specific features of the language in use while, at the same time, trying to keep in mind the text as a whole; and I could tinker to my heart's content with any part of this curriculum, making elaborate sequences of lessons on 'irony' for Year 10, say, which at the time convinced me that systematic, focused study of this sort was the answer.

The great disadvantages with this approach, looking back, were that the students were being led through a syllabus which was totally out of their influence or control, which did not acknowledge the real nature of language acquisition and development and did not recognise the potential of other approaches like the thematic. In fact, when a young teacher joined the department, bringing with her some booklets on such themes as Old Age and School Life, put together by working parties of teachers, which she used to good effect, I tried not to let any of her material or approach influence my curriculum.

The Topic Swamp

At that time there was not much inclination to exploit the opportunities which the thematic approach gave teachers to make the language work, to extend the transactional mode into the potentially rich context of a genuine subject with its concomitant thread of purpose, audience and register. Literature tended to be used to illustrate a social point, the subject of language use was neglected, personal growth was left in the lap of the gods and students ended the study of a theme knowing little more about the given topic than when they started.

If, on the other hand, the thematic approach was being taken so that
• a genuine context for language use was being provided;
• the importance of meaning and communication was being stressed;
• the precise nature of specific interaction was being

153

examined,
then a most worthwhile curriculum was being delivered.

Literary Themes

Some themes that a whole class might follow have, in any case, a distinctly literary or linguistic feel. Themes like Mythology, Fairy Stories, Heroes and Villains could be valuable subjects for study. A programme of work on 'time-slip' novels or 'problem' novels would open up a significant theme of modern young adult fiction for extended class work. Alternatively, work on Dreams or Ghosts or Fantasy, the study of Comedy, Newspapers, Dialects or The Language of Disc-Jockeys or Teachers or Doctors or 'Experts' would invite careful attention to be paid to the way language works and is used.

Themes and Class Readers

It is unlikely that an English teacher would launch into a novel without time being spent creating an interest among the students either for the type of novel about to be read or the theme or period about which the author was writing. If a teacher intends to read *The Grapes of Wrath* to a Year 11 class she might well spend three weeks setting work in motion that relates to the Great Depression, or Odysseys, Quests, The Dust Bowl, Woody Guthrie, Protest Music, topics likely to absorb the students, broaden their appreciation of language and life and stimulate an interest in *The Grapes of Wrath*. So the teacher might see the book as either the culmination, the purpose behind the introductory theme work or as a component of work within a particular theme.

Subject Matter

The theme of War is rich in possibilities for class work because of the literature that might be drawn in, the study of language – euphemism, propaganda, rhetoric, reportage – that might be made and the activities that might be encouraged – debates, role plays, song writing, empathetic work – though it may be too solemn a subject and too far removed from the experiences of the students to be properly manageable or for justice to be done to it. Perhaps themes like Youth, School, Community, Discipline, Nature, Fellow Man – of which War might be an element – Gender, Intolerance, The Welfare State, are more suitable.

154

Class Debate

I watched a class the other day in debate about whether or not the police in Britain should be armed, as part of a theme of Law Enforcement which included the reading of *Nineteen Eighty-Four*. It was a good example of the way a framework of security, in this instance provided by the procedure of a semi-formal debate, can enable students to talk to each other at length with time to make sense of their reactions and feelings and time to reflect on the contributions of others. The teacher and I were able to enjoy the excitement of a discussion that generated its own momentum and thrust, as well as ask the students such questions as why they thought they believed what they did, why they contributed a lot to class discussion, whether they believed they might change their mind during such a talk, what was going on in their head when they remained silent for a long while.

In the context of work on a theme extending over several weeks, this sort of class activity, when it is calm, circumspect and tolerant, is invaluable:
• The students are dealing with important matters.
• They are learning how to interact creatively through the use of language.
• They are finding suitable information, weighing it up, reorganising it and representing it.
• They are seeing how the language says what it says, by making effective use of it.

Visiting Experts

One of the students involved in this debate was a policeman's daughter, who was able to contribute opinions that she had picked up by talking over the subject at home. It might have been even better if the father had been able to come to school to represent his points of view himself, or for a colleague to have come. Visiting experts would provide useful practice in the skills of interviewing, questioning and listening as well as the formal skills of introducing, thanking and reporting back.

Themes of Local Concern

Students in the Midlands have recently been taking issues of local concern for their themes:
• One class has been involved in an investigation of the plans for a proposed coal mine in green belt country near its school;

155

• Another has explored the intentions of the planning committee over the town centre shopping precinct;

• A third has traced the progress of a project to knock down a terrace of Victorian dwelling houses and erect in its place a giant fast-food restaurant;

• A fourth class has researched the history of an area of town called Monkspath, which has recently become a large housing estate but whose name suggests an intriguing past;

• A fifth has looked into the local job situation.

• A sixth has investigated the role of the Central Library in the community.

All these ventures have meant that

• classes have had to leave their schools to go out into their communities to meet people, to research in archives and libraries and council offices, to visit old people's homes, interview people in their houses, talk to councillors, and tape-record conversations;

• material has been gathered, brought back to the classroom to be processed and written up in reports that are classified in the school library;

• letters have been written to local residents, local dignitaries, and to the local paper;

• students have had to draft their written work to suit the situation: register and tone have had to be appropriate, surface features likes spelling, punctuation and handwriting have had to be brought up to scratch so that recipients weren't scandalised;

• students have learned that through their language they can significantly influence people and events;

• students have learned to attach more importance to their local community and their place in it.

At one and the same time, students were absorbed in finding out more about the nature of their community and how it worked, using language in a variety of significant ways, working co-operatively with each other, with their teacher and with local residents, fired with the enthusiasm that comes when you're on the trail of worthwhile knowledge. The work was devised by the teachers, but involved the students because it concentrated their attention on their own environment and had an obvious worthwhile purpose.

Planning by the Students

This kind of activity requires a considerable amount of planning, though the following-up of false trails, the occasional rebuttal from an administrator or a preoccupied resident or the last minute realisation that an intended visit to the old people's home would be insensitive is educationally useful in its own way. The planning, though, does not have to be done by the teacher. Far better for it to be done by the students themselves, because if they do the necessary telephoning, letter writing and organisation of the plan of campaign they will be introduced to other real life language activities and situations.

Cover

Such thematic studies are very worthwhile, and problems of out-of-school supervision and transport, though tiresome, should not curtail them. In most authorities a proforma from the Head Teacher to the parents of students concerned informing them of the proposed excursion and asking for their permission, and a form to the council offices, are sufficient cover. It might also be worth looking to TVE, LEATGS or ESG, or to LMS, for funding to provide a peripatetic teacher or a temporary supply teacher to assist with the supervision of students when they are all out of the classroom, or to give cover for those in the classroom while their classmates are out doing research work.

Extended simulations
Imaginative Involvement

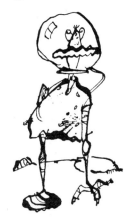

The other day the Year 10 class of students heading for a colleague's classroom was making more than the usual amount of excited noise. His students generally looked forward to English but on this occasion the chatter of enthusiastic expectation was more noticeable than usual. It made me look to my own docile class and wonder where I'd gone wrong. Afterwards, in the staffroom over coffee, I found that he had reached the stage of his current extended simulation when the students were to set off on their holidays. For the last few weeks they had, in role, been planning for this day, deciding on their destinations, designing hotels, writing reports of local conditions, making travel brochures, booking flights and accommodation. When the big day arrived it was as though they really were about to head off to the kind of exotic spot that a teacher can only dream about. They were only dreaming about it too, but their imaginations had been so fired by the work that real adrenalin was flowing.

Use of Language

There are sceptics of the value of classroom-bound simulations, which they see as a very poor second to the real activities engaged in while investigating the role of the local corner shop or the effectiveness of a new traffic system. Rather than being less valid, they seem to be just different, and not very different at that. There is still the need for students to research in order to gather the material which will flesh out the idea. Perhaps more important, there is the subject focus which will provide the range of language activities which can cover the expressive, poetic and transactional modes. Both the out-of-classroom theme approach and the extended simulation offer a means of generating transactional writing because of the various situations which contextualise it. The holiday sequence mentioned above, for example, will naturally give rise to persuasive writing in various tones and for various purposes, argumentative writing, reportage, interrogation of an informal and formal nature, description, euphemism, and so on.

I also watched recently the last stages of a cruise simulation which, after several weeks of the students in role sailing round the Mediterranean, culminated in the captain throwing a party. Again, the classroom was a babble of chatter. Groups sat at tables exchanging small talk, couples danced, the waiters circulated, a gathering of disenchanted holidaymakers lounged by the window, the captain, senior members of the crew and celebrities sat at the high table. Later the captain thanked the crew and complimented them for their hard work and co-operation. The trippers wrote letters to him expressing their gratitude for a safe voyage and detailing their reactions to the holiday for the benefit of future cruisers. Oral and written work operated within a context which provided
• a continuity;
• a specific situation requiring a precise and appropriate use of language;
• a purpose for the work;

158

•a specific audience to receive the communications;
•a will to do it and do it well.

That the adventure took place in the minds of the students seems to me almost a bonus!

Real Situations

But there is a halfway house between the 'real' out-of-classroom theme and the imaginative simulation exercise when, for example, students assume the role of participants in a drama that is actually being enacted somewhere else. In Newbury a large roundabout was being planned in response to parental pressure on the council to improve a notorious stretch of road on which a child had recently been injured. Building the roundabout meant that two public houses would lose part of their forecourt, three private houses would have half of their front gardens taken away, and the rural character of one of the lanes meeting this junction would be lost.

Interacting with each other around this issue were various pressure groups and several experts. Students in the classroom
•assumed specific roles;
•researched into the traffic flow and alternative solutions;
•studied the details of the proposal, the reasons behind it, the most effective design, the sacrifices some would have to make and the material costs;
•found words to express the arguments for and against the scheme;
•in debate, small group discussion, through spokespersons, by letter, article and report in their class version of the local newspaper, came to terms with the complexity of the issue;
•agreed on the most acceptable resolution.

One-off Simulations

There are also shorter versions of simulations, like the commercially available *Tenement* which sets up a situation with each member of class in role as a dweller within the tenement block, an owner or hanger-on, or a member of a local housing or welfare organisation. This sort of simulation is only intended to run for a double period but can be extended if it gives rise to great interest or the issues need more development.

As an introduction to a class reader, simulations are

159

also useful. The teacher might ask: "What if you as a class had to stay in this classroom for an unknown number of days, unable to leave for any reason, with the only visitor someone coming twice a day with minimum rations for your survival, how would you react?" And the students would be encouraged to consider how they would organise themselves; how they would plan the time; how they would make decisions; how they would keep up their spirits. They would discuss how they would feel: excited, free, claustrophobic, lonely. How would they use the visitor? How long could they stand it? For how long could they stay civilised? At which point the teacher would begin to read *Lord of the Flies*. This sort of simulation, in which the students remain themselves but the circumstances change, enables students to empathise more readily with the characters they go on to meet in the class reader.

The Genuine Article

But these short forays into the realm of simulations are slight affairs compared to the genuine article. When the teacher takes a class through several weeks of imaginative engagement in The Desert, The Planet, The Village, The Public School, 10 Downing Street, The Allotment, or on a journey aboard The Orient Express, The Titanic, The Marie Celeste or The Beagle, as well as generating stimulating contexts in which language can function, the students are given the opportunity to live out imaginatively an adventure which they themselves have created. If they have been drawn into the subject by the teacher initially, the creative act of making the story will keep the momentum going.

Making Stories

A feature of these extended simulations is that they exist in a self-contained world, as do many of the novels, say, of Agatha Christie or William Golding. And there is something of a novel about them as the main story develops and the sub-plots intertwine. To begin a simulation of The Village, to take an example, the class would first design the layout, either using a village or local community known to the students or making one up. Each student would then establish in which house he or she lived and develop his or her character, considering

160

past history, appearance, work and personality. Once locality and characters had been created the teacher would introduce a situation or issue.

Telling Stories in Role

One pupil, Sarah, in role, was asked to describe what happened when she saw a ghost as she walked home one night past the old gravel-pits in the village. She described the end of the evening in the pub, the shock of seeing this vague Victorian figure move out over the water and lift its arms beseechingly to the shore, her flight home and her vow never to drink another drop.

She told the story in tiny, telling detail, without hesitation, holding her classmates spellbound by her story and her delivery.

The Value of Extended Simulations

Starting with Sarah's story, the following points about the value of extended simulations can be made:

•Firstly, the power of story-making is so natural and so strong that it will flourish in sympathetic conditions to which a steadily building context contributes.

•Making a story on the spur of the moment, retelling it at a later date, having it reported by word of mouth and in the newspaper draws attention to the circumstances that affect the shaping of a story and its narration, to the alternative ways in which the same story might be told, and to the differences between spoken and written English.

•The qualities of good oral storytelling can be discussed and a reason then provided for a professional storyteller to be engaged by the school.

•Sarah's ghost story was one of a series of stories. In their retelling, stories are often adapted to suit the teller's purpose. The initial facts, however dubious they might be, are heightened, distorted, forgotten or blurred to such an extent that the original might have virtually disappeared. However, the many variations can add to the character of the simulation.

•More stories accrued as the simulation proceeded. There was a move by the private golf club to extend its course to eighteen holes by buying up the gravel-pits frequented over the years by fishermen and courting couples. There was a fire in the newly opened and much-resisted fish and chip shop. Some dubious goings-on behind the scenes of the village poetry competition caused suspicions of favouritism. The story of the village took a backwards step when excavations for a Woolworth's store revealed a Roman site. So the story grew until it became a kind of episodic class novel. If each student's contribution, oral and written, had been put together it would have revealed a remarkable achievement, created out of joint endeavour and energised by co-operative talent.

• Each student is able to succeed in the eyes of his or her peers. Because such a variety of oral, written, dramatic and aesthetic activities can be generated over the weeks, there is no member of the class who would not be able to perform in one or more of them well.

• The teacher, once the simulation is under way, can stimulate whatever language activity might seem appropriate. The poetry competition was instituted simply because it was time for some poetry to be written, and there is no doubt that an extra impetus was given to the composition by the context provided by the village simulation.

• Issues can also be raised and dealt with more rationally because at one remove with all the students in role. Isssues of race and gender can be given a thorough examination within the imagined world of the simulation, given more consideration, viewed from different points of view, even analysed symbolically, as when fishermen in the village netted a strange humanoid creature and the community had to decide what should be done with this 'alien'.

Simulations can be used to deal with social matters, the sort of concerns that form the texture of our communal lives. They can take an open-ended subject like The Village into which can be introduced all manner of topics, or a much more specific subject like The Gardening Competition or The Mental Hospital where one issue is dwelt on for a lengthy period so that a considerable amount of understanding is built up. But they can also be used in the exploration of literature, for example genres like the horror story or the detective story, so that the class can enact its own version and become familiar with a particular story type.

The Student as Author

Throughout these descriptions of simulations the teacher has been depicted as the grand designer of the enterprise, but she can hand this responsibility to one or more of the students whose task it then becomes to plan a series of incidents out of which a story evolves, enabling the remaining students to use language in a variety of ways. Alternatively, students can be encouraged to take over the unfolding story as the mood or inclination takes them so that the whole enterprise really does become self-generating. A judicious questioning on the part of the teacher will enable the lead to be taken in turn round the class, the authorship of the story being assumed for a time then handed on. So the unfolding story becomes even richer as it grows out of the interests and imaginations of different members of the class.

CHAPTER FOUR

TOWARDS STUDENT CHOIC[...]

Students' language skills develop when they compose, in speech and writing, for a variety of significant purposes with deliberate care; when they read with discernment and listen attentively. The energy required for such involvement can be released if students are able to choose some of their English activities after open negotiation with their teachers. This chapter looks briefly at the educational value of students making choices in the classroom, describes how a degree of choice can be introduced and concludes with strategies deliberately aimed at furthering and fostering choice.

General Principles
Why Choice?

For students to have the opportunity to choose the piece of work they are going to do next is fundamentally educative: if the choice is made carefully it involves
• evaluating;
• comparing;
• speculating;
• looking at specifics while keeping in mind a whole programme;
• considering balance, breadth and relevance;
• considering what would be valuable, beneficial or ultimately rewarding to do as against what might appear to be easy or fun to do.

Various considerations would be taken into account if the student and teacher were to discuss together what his next piece of work might be:
• How demanding were the last pieces of work?
• In what way were they demanding? Emotionally? Intellectually?
• Has there been too much written work recently?
• Has there been too much drama work recently?
• Has the student been working on his own for too long?
• Are the requirements of the National Curriculum being met?

Sometimes, though, the selection of the next piece of work would be a very straightforward matter:
• it will grow out of the last piece;
• it will arise from the current private reader or an experience at home;

• it will be prompted by work a classmate has done or is doing;

• there is need for some relaxation with a less demanding activity.

Making a sensible decision as to the nature of the next piece of work would be difficult for those who were not used to choosing, but it is important that those students particularly should be encouraged to think carefully about their curriculum and gain more experience in making choices. All students reaching adolescence have to face decision-making of one kind or another, some which will significantly affect their lives. Teachers can provide a secure context in which students will learn how to go about making confident, deliberate decisions and become more independent and effective in the school itself and beyond.

Ownership

Once the choice of the next piece has been made, the student will feel that he has some stake in the work. Instead of there being an imposition of an unwelcome task, he has identified what might next be done and the task has become his own. This simple knowledge, that he is doing this work because he has chosen it, means that the responsibility to do it well is his; and if he really feels a sense of ownership he will attempt to do it as well as he can. This feeling may not be apparent in the early attempts at the self-selection of tasks, because some students will not have experienced for a time the intrinsic interest that language work has. Once the sense of involvement begins to develop, though, and the awareness that he has himself determined what he is going to do grows, he will begin to want to do this work well. He will take a pride in it in a way that he seldom would have done when an assignment had been imposed on him.

A piece of work might be hard, but if it is your own and you have set your own targets and found your own reason for doing it the work becomes more like play. And the absorption that play allows is the right condition for learning.

Practicalities

A tension existed throughout the last chapter between

165

my descriptions of full class activities and my feelings that each of those activities might be more satisfactorily pursued by small groups of students who had opted for them. A group of between two and six students might form out of a common interest in reading *The Nature of the Beast* by Janni Howker, for example, and this group could decide in consultation with the teacher how the book would be read: at home, round the group in class time, straight through or section by section; and could devise activities to be carried out during the reading and plan ways for an understanding and appreciation to be gained. By this means the process of selection, reading and response would be in the hands of the students: the learning that took place would be more natural, and, because more personal and intuitive, probably more profound. As for thematic work which might necessitate fieldwork activities beyond the classroom, how much easier it would be to organise if only a handful of students were involved. And how much more fully each member of the group would be able to take part in the planning, the investigation and the processing of information.

An Active Audience

If students did work in groups or as individuals on a range of optional activities, plenary sessions could be periodically held so that progress could be reported on and finished pieces of work presented or performed to the rest of the class. Such a reporting-back could serve many purposes:

•On the social level it would help sustain a class cohesion and build mutual respect.

•It would enable the interests and achievements of each member of the class to become better known and acknowledged.

•A goal would have been set for the work, so that the students were aiming high to satisfy themselves and make the product good enough for the scrutiny of their classmates.

•Skills of reporting back and presentation techniques would be developed.

•When a presentation was done well this would invite praise and build self-esteem.

•Participants whose presentation had been received with

approval and helpful evaluation would be likely to do even better next time.

• A sense of collaborative enterprise would grow.

• For the rest of the class a body of information, a work of art or a response would have been shared, and there would have been the opportunity to react sympathetically and with constructive criticism, as long as the teacher had managed to establish a positive and supportive ethos in the classroom.

Teachers' Time

And from the teacher's point of view to have students working in groups on a variety of activities would enable her to use her time more effectively. Some groups, because of the nature of the work they were doing, would not require much of her time, while others would benefit from considerable teacher input. Where students were absorbed in their work and able to make significant progress on their own, a passing comment, a redirecting or challenging question or a few words of encouragement would be sufficient: to spend more time in such circumstances might be unnecessary, even counter-productive. On the other hand, where material was unfamiliar, the task particularly demanding, or where new concepts were being tackled, it would be necessary for the teacher to put in a considerable amount of time.

The Beginnings of Choice
Students' Inclination

The teacher is often pushed into taking the first steps towards allowing some student choice of the English curriculum by the students themselves. The student who has read *Go Well, Stay Well* by Toeckey Jones and does not want to read it again when it is selected by the teacher as the class reader might ask to read something else during this time. The student who has got halfway through *One-eyed Cat* by Paula Fox on his own and wants to continue it in his English lesson while other students do their classwork might be allowed to read quietly, and, having finished, do some work on it himself, perhaps persuading some of his friends to read it too. The teacher is able to accommodate individuals into the scheme of things and let the process develop, while maintaining a firm sense of control over the whole class's activities.

But once students recognise that an element of choice is

167

permissible, more will probably want to take advantage of it. One will want to do some expressive writing on something going on at home that he is anxious about; another will want to work with a friend to produce some short stories about a common interest; a group will want to do some drama work.

Teachers' Initiatives

Students' own inclinations, then, might be the start of optional work in the English classroom but it is, in any case, the stock in trade of most teachers to offer a series of choices to the students while they are reading or when they have finished a class reader. Such a system merely needs extending so that the interest generated by a critical or empathetic essay, or further reading, or research, is allowed to develop.

Once the class is engaged in responses to the class reader, the teacher is free to work with individual students to support them in their current work and help them plan a short programme of their own. If the teacher is used to giving students a weekly silent reading period this, too, might be a time to talk at some length with individuals, encouraging them to consider what they would most like to do.

The Menu

If the teacher does offer a list of options none of them need be denied any of the students, unless an individual's programme of work has been so weighted towards a certain type of activity that important areas of language study are being neglected, in which case the teacher might make strong recommendations that the student should consider planning a more balanced programme. There should, though, in a mixed ability class, be the full range of options open to all students so that the least academic would be able, for example, to attempt an intellectually demanding literature criticism essay if he so wished; and indeed, from time to time, perhaps he should be positively encouraged to do so.

The format of the literary essay – the main point, the evidence, the comments on the evidence leading to the next point – offers a structure to the student's response which can have a releasing, supporting, stimulating effect, and the skills required in the writing of a literary essay ought to be fostered in all students. The ability to make a point, marshal, organise and select material, evaluate, compare and contrast may not always be apparent in a student but they will remain underdeveloped unless he is given the opportunity to exercise them and his teacher encourages the necessary self-belief.

By the same token the student who shows a lot of academic potential would not be expected to choose invariably the intellectually demanding option. No one type of response or activity should be perceived as by its nature superior in the mixed ability classroom, or a hierarchy of achievement would quickly become established which would cause social cohesion and mutual respect to dissipate quickly.

The Jigsaw Classroom

To build self-confidence and a sense of independence in learning the teacher might use such strategies as the jigsaw classroom, a scheme in which the teacher organises her students systematically. The outcomes in terms of learning about
• the subject under study;
• language and learning;
• oneself as an independent learner;
make it very useful.

Students are grouped four to a table and the students at each table are lettered A, B, C and D. The task is identified by the teacher – let's say we are going to learn about the history of the locality. Four aspects of this general topic are defined:
• legends relating to the area;
• important local personnages;
• building developments over the last hundred years;
• the growth of amenities.

The A students are allocated legends, the Bs local personnages, the Cs building developments and the Ds amenities.

Next, the students are asked to group according to their letters and plan how they will set about gathering information on their specified subject:
• They may have to remain within the classroom;
• Perhaps they can use the school library;
• Interviewing members of the school staff may be permissible.

169

•They may be able to leave the school premises to visit local institutions.

The period of research may take one double period or it may stretch over several weeks, depending on the nature of the topic and the self-motivation of the students. Once the research has been completed, and the students might be expected to work collaboratively with all the As together or independently, the original groups of A, B, C and D students reconvene. The newly acquired expertise is presented to the other three students at the table who question their tutors to glean as much information as they can.

This is the basic pattern, but all kinds of variations are possible. For example, when the students are able to cope with more freedom they might determine the sub-topics for research themselves; they might, indeed, develop such responsibility for their learning that they decide what the actual subject for investigation will be. Nor does the whole class have to be involved. One or two groups of students can work within the jigsaw structure while the remainder work in other ways.

Reporting Back

Independence as a learner and a greater self-confidence in using the language can be fostered by a simple means of asking a student or group of students to find out about something for the rest of the class. The teacher might ask a student to go to the library to research a subject, visit another classroom to find out what colleagues think or conduct a survey among members of staff. On his return the student would organise his material and then present it to his class. This activity causes the minimum of disruption and unobtrusively but effectively gives students a sense that they can be the masters of their own destinies: they have the wherewithal to learn on their own and the capability to pass on their learning to others.

Strategies to Encourage Choice
Initial Rounds

A session could start with the students and their teacher all seated on their chairs in a circle facing each other, the tables back against the wall, as described at the end of Chapter One and illustrated in Example C. If the teacher is taking a class activity that will extend over a few sessions she might ask those who are already engaged in their own work to tell the rest where they have got to before leaving the circle to continue with it. She can then carry on with her reader, her thematic work or whatever she is working on in her core syllabus with the rest of the class.

But if her core syllabus is at this time a series of lessons each contained within one session, she may extend this period of whole class discussion by sharing news from about the school or community, inviting comments, anecdotes, points of view; she may read a poem or a short story to the full class so that it can be enjoyed by all. Then those who have their own work in progress and with them and, after careful negotiation, those who wish to begin some work of their own choice, will leave the circle. When they have left, the remaining students can work with the stimulus material in whatever ways the teacher has devised, and there will probably be a range of activities on offer. In this way, after about fifteen minutes, individuals and groups are scattered about the classroom involved in various kinds of work.

Final Rounds

Some time before the close of the session the circle could be reconvened and each student in turn asked to make a comment on what has been achieved in the last hour. One or two students might have something finished and ready for presentation and they will take the opportunity to share their work with the rest. The tape, illustration or piece of writing will be shared by the other students, who will get some of the benefit of their classmates' work as they experience their achievements.

The main purpose of this 'round' is for students to get used to the idea of reflecting on the value of the work they have done, to ask questions of themselves like:
•How well am I getting on with this project?
•Is it better than the last one I did?
•What has been the most useful part of it?
•Has the audience's reaction been what I intended it to be?
•What have I learned today?
•Am I becoming a better learner?

It is a short time for reflection when the thoughts of one student can rub off on another so that each becomes

171

increasingly skilled at analysing the value of his work and the work of others. And this process, in turn, affects how well students are able to direct their own work through the exercise of choice, because they learn to recognise, for example, that certain superficially attractive options don't necessarily give much satisfaction.

The final 'round' also has a vital disciplinary function. When there are various activities going on in and around the classroom, some noisy and verging on the unruly from time to time, and when students are scattered in ones, pairs and small groups, it is essential that the session ends on a calm note, that the last experiences of the English classroom are quiet and reflective. At this time loose ends can be tied up, writers' blocks can be discussed, successes enjoyed and the considered comments of each member of the class demonstrated to be valued by peers and the teacher.

Negotiation

"$?_*!!_{-;}?_{-,}!$"

And it is a time when shared enthusiasms can spark interest in others so that at the next round when the class meets again there might be other students who wish to propose a programme of work to the teacher, and this is when the skills of negotiation – making the case and accepting the verdict – can be exercised.
• The regularity with which the round occurs carries with it implicitly the message that this is the forum in which the discussion over curriculum takes place.
• It is where the major problems of decision-making and progress in work are addressed.
• It is where, as far as possible, the requirements for the session are identified and organised.
This is to make sure that once students with their own work have left the full group with whom the teacher is working, she is not besieged by students outside the circle interrupting her with one request after another.

Private Readers and Diaries

To ensure that such interruptions are kept to the minimum, it is very helpful if the English department establishes a policy that every student in the school has the responsibility to bring with him to every English session his private reader, the novel that he has chosen from the class, school or local library and is currently reading. When the time comes, as it inevitably will with some students, that the chosen work does not seem quite as gripping as it had promised to be and they run out of steam, they then have a book that they can turn to.

They might also be encouraged to use a section of their English file for making personal jottings: odd remarks they hear, lines from a book they like, some thoughts on something that is worrying them, little comments and half-formed ideas, or regular reflections on their learning. For those who would prefer exercise books for their private records of feelings and observations, these could be available.

These two strategies need never become redundant because they are so worthwhile in themselves, a natural and constructive accompaniment to the other activities that take place in the English classroom. There is probably nothing more valuable that a student can do in English from a language study and a personal growth point of view than to read a book of his choice or use writing as a means of learning more about his own circumstances.

Three Stages

Up to this point students' choice has been encouraged on three fronts:
•The teacher offers a range of alternative activities after each stimulus and students are encouraged to take seriously the business of selection and later of evaluation.
•Secondly, enterprising students who express a wish to do a particular activity which runs parallel to the class work, as with the student who has read the class novel *Of Mice and Men* and wants to read instead *Cannery Row* or, come to that, *Shane* or some James Thurber short stories, is encouraged to do so.
•Thirdly, even if what the student wishes to do has no bearing whatsoever on the class work but is considered by him and the teacher to be a worthwhile activity at that particular time he would be allowed, indeed encouraged, to do it.

Small Group Role Play

The teacher could also employ two further strategies for setting up alternatives and developing her students' ability to make considered choices. The usefulness of a small room, a walk-in cupboard or a stairwell was recognised in Chapter One. It can provide a haven of silence when most of the class are indulging in dramatic goings-on or it can contain a rowdy discussion group if the other class members and the teacher need to consider the state of their nerves. At the start of each session, or whenever during the course of the term it seems appropriate, the teacher might ask for a group of four volunteers to devise a role play. Ways of influencing the composition of the group to ensure things like a mix of sex, ability and fresh faces will be described in the next chapter. On the inside of his English file each student might stick a list of language functions:

Tease	Criticise	Report
Discourage	Flannel	Plead
Excuse	Explain	Boast
Convert	Demonstrate	Persuade
Humour	Describe	Reminisce
Moderate	Apologise	Speculate
Compromise	Sympathise	Propose
Preach	Cajole	Predict
Interrupt	Encourage	Yearn
Praise	Remonstrate	Order
Introduce	Condemn	Specify
Cheer up	Soothe	Disabuse
Evaluate	Define	Dissuade
Judge	Review	Dismiss
Summarise	Decry	Flatter
Mock	Satirise	Support

The self-selected group of students could be asked to choose one of the above and create a play taking that function as its main theme. If it chose Persuade the group would be expected to devise a situation in which one or more of the characters had to use all their powers of persuasion to gain their objective. The victims should resist the pressure for all they were worth, so that those persuading would have to dig deeply into their resources of language and personality, and in so doing learn more about the nature of that language function and develop their own linguistic powers and self-confidence. Having decided on a function the group would go off into the small room to work at it and at the end of the session re-emerge with a tape of the scene or a play to be performed before the rest of the class during the final round. Once the presentation had taken place, classmates would be invited to join in discussion about it so that in this period of analysis all members of the class would gain.

The Ideas Box

Text books might be available in the classroom to give students ideas for a programme of work, and they could be supplemented by an Ideas Box. This could take the form of a plastic container kept on one of the tables, containing ideas cards in classified sections composed by the class teacher or by the department working together. These ideas cards would probably not be as attractive as the pages of modern course or source books but they could be illustrated and laminated so that they are visually exciting and durable. Their virtues are two-fold:

• They can be representative of the class teacher's free and spontaneous imagination. Something she has just read in a text book on English teaching or language development can provide the seed for a stimulating ideas card. An idea from a lesson, a thought in the bath, an observation on a run can furnish a series of cards, even a new classification section. The very existence of an ideas box would prompt and foster one-offs and sequences of lessons and encourage the teacher to be steadily generating and holding on to creative ideas for language work.

• The ideas cards can be of very local and topical interest. They can reflect the interests of the teacher and/or the department that compiles them so that they are very much an extension of a particular personality or group of personalities. Some of them could focus on local figures, local issues, the concerns or enthusiasms of members of the school, clubs, fads, issues of controversy. So some of the work that emanates from the ideas box can be seen to have a relevance and implication specific to the school or even the clsssroom where it is located.

Other sources for ideas worth tapping are colleagues in local schools, student teachers and the students in Years 10 and 11 themselves. The latter group may have plenty of suggestions for subject or skills related activities and

175

Example of Ideas Card

FEATURES OF POEMS: VERBS 67

THE FOX CAPE

The fox runs!
Flame-thrown it snaps the frosted stalks
① the white winter bracken.

This one ② the dressing chair
of a decorated lady.
Its overblown black fur crowds
the cardboard snout, an unfamiliar wig.
The beads that ③ out peer and frown.
Grey flecks, black silk at the back ...
no fox, then. Yet a meagre claw
④ the dainty dangling foot.
Something ⑤ once.

Did this fox
⑥ the morning with its raucous throat?
With a scream of joining this mated
not with her red dog, but with a sharp pellet
that ⑦ her warm blood, left
empty flesh first stiff, then dry
then bone and no skin.

Where
is tonight's fox, fluid over the grass?
What bark?
What, is it wary?
What perfume does it ⑧ upon the window wind?

(Heather Harrison)

① browns bends
  sears witters

② covers adorns
  drapes graces

③ eye gleam
  stare pop

④ tips hooks
  ends frills

⑤ pounced trod
  tiptoed lived

⑥ waken rouse
  tear stir

⑦ silvered stilled
  chilled clogged

⑧ sniff smell
  receive catch

AIM: To understand more about the themes of this poem by looking very closely at the poet's use of verbs.

DIRECTIONS:
1. Ask someone in the group to read out the poem.
2. Read it to yourself a couple of times.
3. Discuss it as a group and begin to select from the options on the right the verbs that you feel fit best.
4. You may either select the verbs privately and then compare them or choose each one as a group.
5. When you have finished, see if all the verbs you have chosen form a consistent theme.
6. Are all the verbs equally effective?
7. Do you want to learn the poem?

176

could even be encouraged to produce, in groups, ideas cards for other English classes, based on a scheme of work in hand or a novel, play or poem they are involved with.

It need not be burdensome to put an ideas box together. As part of her routine preparatory work, the teacher might make up one sheet over a period of time, say a week or a fortnight, so that there was a steadily growing bank of ideas cards in the box, or she might just use ideas as they occur to her. Of course the teacher needs to be aware of the constraints of copyright laws when putting together her own resources.

Missing the Core

In this system of running the English classroom once students have left the circle to continue or commence work of their choice the teacher tends to be left with something like half the class who wish to 'be taught', to follow the core course designed by her. It will not be the same students each session, for some will finish their own work and rejoin the core while others will be moved to strike out independently for a while. I do not believe it matters that 'good lessons' introduced by the teacher as part of her course are being missed by opters-out: progress towards greater language accomplishment is not a linear development. We learn through use and by sharing each other's practice, so what we miss in one setting we meet somewhere else, not necessarily in the classroom, and the regular presentations of students' achievements create a very rich and varied language experience in which the whole class can grow.

Drawing the Class Together Again

And when the teacher for whatever reason decides that the time has come to draw the class back together and have a period of full class teaching she could
• stop any more optional activities hiving off so that as students complete an option they rejoin the core;
• set a date by which all optional activities were to be completed and require students who overran that date to complete their work at home;
• if things were going badly, ask the students either to abandon their optional activities or finish them for homework and institute full class activity immediately.

CHAPTER FIVE

THE TEACHER-MANAGER

Despite all the pressures and pitfalls, optimistic teachers continue to search for a means of unlocking the energies and abilities of each of their students. That elusive key involves good management – of the curriculum, class and group discussion, the class and the classroom – and is the subject of this chapter. Some of the difficulties that teachers face daily are discussed and an idealised description of a class at work is given.

A Working Classroom
The Core

The English teacher has just finished a reading of *The Loneliness of the Long Distance Runner* as part of a series of work on 'different points of view'. She has been working with a group of fourteen students and during the reading there has been no movement to or from her group; for this time it has been necessary for opters-out to continue with their work and the core group to remain committed to the book. She has asked the floating teacher, the peripatetic support teacher, to work with the opters-out while she takes her core onto the sports field, where the fourteen take the parts of the runner, three other racers, three Borstal Headteachers and their wives, three parents of the inmates and a reporter from the local newspaper. When they have enacted the end of the race they return to the classroom, the support teacher is able to move to another class, and the fourteen students, on the basis of the reading and the role play, now write their accounts of the race for their local newspaper from the point of view of the characters they have each assumed.

The Rest

Of the remaining fifteen members of this class, one is reading *The Haunting* by Margaret Mahy and one is writing a letter to the vet thanking her for nursing his cat. Four students are sitting around two tables blocked together planning work on the poem *The Ballad of Charlotte Dymond* by Charles Causley. They have been thinking about the poem for over a week and are considering either a dramatisation of the murder or a series of four illustrations of the main episodes. At another blocked table four more students are planning stories for their feeder junior school. The class was recently visited by a group of children from this school who commissioned four science fiction stories from them. The students are agreeing on the characters that will be common to all the stories and discussing incidents that will give their writing contrast but also compatibility.

The remaining three activities taking place in this classroom refer to particular students I have taught or heard about. My main purpose in giving this description of a classroom in action is to provide a background against which to discuss the teacher's role, but I want with the next three activities to underline the significance of the student choice principle.

Theresa is writing poetry. She has been doing this for two or three weeks now, and although she will leave school with a lower than average assessed grade, she has a flair with words and an unusual awareness of the flow of time. Her poems are on the classroom walls; they have appeared in magazines published in the school and her classmates recognise the ability she has. I met her three years after she left school shopping in Swindon. She was working in a local factory and still writing poetry as a hobby.

Anna is writing a series of short stories. She is a very literate girl who reads a lot on her own and is interested in exploring different ways of telling a story.

Four difficult boys have asked to devise a role play involving a street gang and a young Pakistani shopkeeper – I heard this account from Chris Searle, the teacher whose students wrote *Stepney Words* – and with severe misgivings the teacher has allowed them to go ahead. They are occupying the little room. When the time comes for the improvisation to be performed in the final 'round' before the class, the teacher is far from relaxed. Although she knows the students have taken this task seriously, she is still greatly relieved and delighted to find that instead of fighting the shopkeeper and stealing his takings the gang befriends him. When she asks how this development came about she is told that as they were making up the play, imagining their characters' backgrounds and home circumstances and creating dialogue, they 'got to know' the shopkeeper, and the four characters became friends.

I don't know any story that reinforces my faith in the

creative art, real student interaction or the value of students negotiating their work and sharing outcomes as strongly as this one does.

The Reality

Of course, English teachers would live to a ripe old age if the serene classroom described above were routine! And things will, in reality, always be going wrong to subvert this harmonious holiday-snap depiction. Tape recorders break down inconveniently, the eye doctor arrives out of the blue, the support teacher doesn't turn up or gets played up, a couple or more of the students for a very good reason or for none you can discern behave very badly, or the improvisation degenerates into a maul. Yet by basing the classroom work on the students' own choices, the dangers of coercion and alienation have been eased. If the habitual ways of working in this classroom,
•the 'rounds';
•the one-to-one support;
•the genuine and serious interest in each student's work;
•the shared performances;
•the evaluations;
are seen to underline the importance of each student and of language study, most students will respond for most of the time. When the teacher, expressing genuine interest in the student's anecdotes, responds with her own, and when the student's careful work has an explicit purpose, is warmly received, sensitively discussed, perhaps displayed, the student's sense of his worth grows, pride in his work increases and he looks forward to English sessions as a time that promises some sense of engagement, productivity and fulfilment.

Managing the Core Syllabus
The Core Syllabus

What comprises the core syllabus will be a matter very personal to the teacher, for this spine of work will represent her underlying philosophy of what should be offered on the English curriculum. It is important, whether the teacher is working with the whole class or only the half or so who have not opted out, that the core syllabus should offer
•literature from different times and different cultures, with plenty of time given for students' own and varied responses;

180

• the opportunity to write at different lengths, in different modes and always for an explicit purpose;
• the opportunity to talk and listen across the formal-informal continuum about issues that they feel to be significant and in ways that lead to real collaborative learning.

One or more of the different views as listed by the Cox Committee, the
• Personal Growth
• Cross Curriculum
• Adult Needs
• Cultural Heritage
• Cultural Analysis

view, will be emphasised, depending on the particular beliefs of the teacher, but it is important for the sake of the students' broad education that all are represented; and, in fact, their representation is specified by the National Curriculum programmes of study which reflect them all.

Towards Role Plays

I moved away from a determinedly sequential syllabus because of a growing interest in role plays and the increasing difficulty I had in keeping a broad curriculum while trying to concentrate for a length of time on a particular feature like narrative, description or character, or trying to keep a whole text in mind while focusing attention on one stylistic feature. Looking at a recent syllabus of mine there is a full class role play to start the year followed by work on the traditional ballad using poems like *The Unquiet Grave*, *The Withered Arm* ; the balladic novella by Thomas Hardy, some of Charles Causley's ballads, *Grauballe Man* by Seamus Heaney, and another role play, this one an extended simulation based on the building of the stone circles of Avebury, a stone age site twenty miles down the road from the school. Several linking threads might be drawn out here. The ballad form, treatment and tradition is one; imagery, I remember, was another.

More Student Involvement

At the end of this term we did a role play based on an imaginary journey to Transylvania during which the class broke into three groups, each one led by a student whose task it was to sustain the adventure by taking over the

181

teacher's role of introducing varied and worthwhile language activities in a story sequence. One of these was successful, the other two quickly ground to a halt, but the experience was sufficiently invigorating to push me towards a more student-orientated approach.

Slanting the material to meet the requirements of a sequential syllabus distorted the selection process itself and the students' response to it, imposing quite unnecessary restrictions on a subject which, under sympathetic and knowledgeable tuition, would stimulate development by its own nature. I still felt that short sequences of lessons on, say, 'the narrative voice' or 'ways of telling a story', on 'description' or, more specifically, 'imagery' or 'the use of the senses', even on 'rhythm' or 'irony' were valuable, but, increasingly, that the students should be encouraged simply to experience the language by reading, writing, talking and listening, using the language with commitment to the task in hand and that then, with a teacher in the background mindful of her role in the learning process and focusing the students' attention on their language activity, with her breadth of reading and knowledge of language development to inform her interventions, the students would learn.

Managing Student Discussion
The Dominant Talker in Class Discussion

With full class discussions the problems have more to do with the students who contribute too much than those who remain silent despite cajoling, soothing or provocation. As long as the topic for discussion is suitably available, open to anecdote, speculation, development of ideas, inviting of response and the teacher's questioning low-key – only obtrusive when there is clearly a need to bring in someone whose contribution is not being paid attention to – the quiet student might be left alone. Students with quiet natures shouldn't be made to feel that they must speak: the teacher should aim to create a supportive atmosphere that will not threaten the shy student and, if such a one does say something, to attempt subtly to draw him out. As long as the silent one is listening to what is going on there is a good chance that he will be learning at least as much as the more vociferous students whose inclination might be to perform rather than consider.

182

It would be hard to run a class discussion without naturally garrulous students but it is a pity when they cannot make their contribution, set the ball rolling, add the occasional elaborated comment and be otherwise content to leave the floor to others. Only by the teacher
- allowing plenty of practice in full class discussion;
- reiterating the value of active listening;
- emphasising the importance of others' opinions;
- stressing and illustrating how wisdom grows through the assimilation of others' points of view;
- giving time for reflection on the reasons for the success or otherwise of a class discussion;
- playing back for analysis tapes of class talk

can the students' appreciation of the art of discussion grow. Ironically if the teacher relinquishes her role as orchestrator of full class discussion so that her students have more scope to shape it, the dominant student is sometimes cast by himself or by his classmates in her place, in which case he does the job far less effectively than the teacher. He becomes more the focus of the discussion than the teacher ever was.

One way out of this predicament is through small group discussion.

The Dominant Talker in Small Groups

If the teacher tends to work with all her students following the same activity she will need, in a small group talk session, to pay considerable attention to the composition of the groups. The incorrigibly dominant students might be put together in the same group. They might be separated. They might or might not be asked to chair a group. If they are, they will have to accept a specific function. If they are not, they will have to learn to work to someone else.

The Joker

As much of a bother to the teacher as the inveterate talker is the compulsive and inopportune joker, who will pun or grimace at every quasi-opportunity with almost pathological regularity. More sensitive, delicate, risky, original buds of conversation are nipped by this student than any teacher would want to lie awake counting. The solution must rest in the teacher helping the students to recognise the nature of discussion, the way it works, and the kind of behaviour the participants need to endorse if it is to flourish and achieve its ends. Tapes of talk can be provided for analysis, students' own discussions can be played back for comment in a 'round' and if the evaluation is done sensitively, the prerequisite that the teacher must insist on, then the joker might recognise the damage that his overweaning sense of humour has unwittingly done.

Some teachers ask their students to determine a set of ground rules for small group discussion. These, made up by the students, are adhered to by them, continually monitored and revised, so that as well as helping with the current discussions they are providing a means of learning more about the way discourse works. The teacher will not wish for great solemnity around the tables and a well-timed joke will contribute greatly to the talk, but an ill-judged wisecrack or an over-dominant speaker will ruin it. And this can be frustrating, for the students and for the teacher. I have known students weep because they have been unable to talk to each other properly: a classmate has mocked them, put them down too fiercely, argued against them with such force that the torrent of words and the power of personality have reduced them to tears. For some students the drama of the small group discussion is such that their adrenalin flows and their output of language is so much more vigorous than they achieve in their relatively colourless written work. These students thrive in oral situations (and for the teacher there is the challenge of how these powers of communication can be reflected in their written work), but the consequence of their intense involvement should not be the acute discomfiture of other students: self-awareness is crucial to all successful talk.

The Composition of Small Groups

As a general rule students will probably talk to better effect if they are with their friends; if the teacher is operating a choice-based system in the classroom the problem of composition will seldom arise, though it does when a number of the class is delegated for small group talk on a language function as described in Chapter Four. A register could then be kept of who has last done this activity and with whom. The next student on the list could

184

then be asked to choose three others to work with him, but not three who have worked with him on this exercise recently. The same sort of procedure might be used for the selection of groups when the whole class is in group work. It overcomes the difficulty of the unpopular one or two that sometimes exist in a class. "We don't want him, thank you very much!" is not a good start to a co-operative learning situation. It helps, too, if the size of the group varies: four seems to be the optimum number according to conventional wisdom, but paired work is often the most appropriate and three, five and six students can work to good effect, particularly with role play and thematic activities.

The Role of the Teacher in Small Group Discussion

As second in the English department, with little appreciation of the finer points of classroom management or the role of the teacher, I used to struggle with small group activities in a cramped terrapin, thankfully some distance from the rest of the school. With only an implicit belief in the ideas of Douglas Barnes I tolerated an inordinate hubbub of noise as lesson after lesson I threw a poem or a topic at each of seven or eight groups and expected them instantly to get their teeth into it. The students would have had no introduction to the text to speak of, and no inkling from me of the purpose behind the activity. Needless to say, these weren't very valuable sessions. I lurched from one group to another trying to keep discussion on task, only to hear the last students I had attended clatter back to the events that would capture their all too obvious energies that night. I saw my role as nudging the students towards specific insights, as this transcript of a small group discussion on *American Primitive* by William Jay Smith shows:

American Primitive

Look at him there in his stovepipe hat,
His high-top shoes, and his handsome collar;
Only my Daddy could look like that,
And I love my Daddy like he loves his Dollar.

The screen door bangs, and it sounds so funny –
There he is in a shower of gold;

185

His pockets are stuffed with folding money,
His lips are blue, and his hands feel cold.

He hangs in the hall by his black cravat,
The ladies faint, and the children holler:
Only my Daddy could look like that,
And I love my Daddy like he loves his Dollar.

William Jay Smith

John: I think he's ... er ... got ... er ... he got ... er ...
very superior ... he acts superior ... you know, his ... he
makes his wife all sort of timid and that ... and they all
sort of ...

Teacher: But they seem to be ...

John: ... stand back and worship him, sort of thing ...

Teacher: There's more than one lady there.

John: Yeah, well ... maybe he shouts at them every
morning ...

Michael: Perhaps he ...

John: All superior.

Michael: Perhaps ... perhaps he went out ... he just went
out and he's come back in now and he's going to do his
wife in or something ...

Teacher: You're ... you're just guessing really. I mean,
the poem says a lot. I think really that we haven't
looked at ... em ... what about 'He hangs in the hall by
his black cravat'? What does that actually mean?

Michael: It almost gives the impression that he's been
hung or hanged.

Teacher: Well, what do you mean, 'almost does'?

Michael: Well, 'He hangs in the hall by his black
cravat', well, yeah ... he's been hung because then it
says 'the children holler'.

Teacher: John?

John: I think he's lingering by his cravat. You know
... he's took his stud (?) off and he's standing there ...

Michael: I reckon he's been hung because 'He hangs in
the hall by his black cravat, The ladies faint and the
children holler'. Say if the ladies ... and the ladies had
seen him they would have fainted (*unintelligible*) ...

Teacher: What do you think about this suggestion then?

John: I think it would have carried on a little bit
longer on that point, really. If he's been hung or shot or

...   186

Teacher: Did it tie up with anything that's happened earlier on in the poem?

John: Not really, no.

Teacher: No? What about 'His lips are blue and his hands feel cold'?

Michael: That gives the impression that he's ... kind of dead ...

John: (*makes a remark, unintelligible because of extraneous classroom noise*)

Michael: ... Yeah, because when you ... when you die you go all stiff don't you? It gives the impression he's stiff, in the poem.

Teacher: Mm ... and what else?

(*Pause*)

Michael: Yeah, his hands feel cold because when a dead body's dead he's ... the whole body's cold innit?

John: Is that what it's supposed to be?

These students had a most unattractive room, a poem that had no context provided by the teacher, the noise of the other groups not at that moment subjected by the teacher's direct presence; they also had any opportunity to assume control of their discussion and thereby the poem and their appreciation of it wrested from them by my determination to move them to an understanding that would satisfy me.

When the discovery is made, one of the group, so cowed by this technique of the teacher's to lead them by the nose to the desired insight, says wearily: "Is that what it's supposed to be?" (Will you leave us alone now?) So by dint of direct pressure and persistent urging some jerky discussion can be set up, but the process is artificial, almost dishonest – it is not the teacher's achievement or the student's, it is a tacitly agreed construction: I'll pretend that it's your discovery if you pretend to be interested!

eal Talk

Too often what passes for discussion in the classroom is only a lifeless imitation of the real thing. Students go through the motions of talk in a desultory and aimless fashion, revealing nothing, exploring nothing, learning nothing. The task, being imposed, does not impinge on them and the talk, consequently, lacks drive.

187

But the real talk will come as soon as the students become engrossed by the problems posed by the task in hand. When the students are involved in a group activity leading to a definite outcome or product, discussion is naturally generated and it tends to be characterised by intense, urgent bursts of talk, by sporadic, excited attempts at finding agreements, solutions, ways forward. And if the work has been self-selected – which will result in a range of activities going on at any one time – and if discussion is only taking place in pockets around the classroom, the teacher is able, by her mere presence, to help sustain it, recognising that it is in the nature of discourse that talkers will wish from time to time to take the discussion away from what is strictly – or even loosely – relevant.

And if behind all the activities in the classroom is a recognition that the subject under study is 'the use of language', how we use it and how we make intellectual and emotional sense of it, and if the students have been able to enjoy the pleasures of a well-told story, the goal of a particular discussion might effectively be no more or less than to discuss *American Primitive*. Students might wish the task to be left at that, or they might prefer, and at times need, a more direct question like: What is the relationship between the child and the father? In what ways does the chorus change its meaning from verse one to verse three? or How can twelve lines mean so much? Either way, they are much more inclined to learn and therefore to talk meaningfully if the teacher keeps her distance and doesn't intrude unnecessarily on the process.

Managing the Students
Vaudeville

An extrovert teacher can win over rowdy students by being even more ebullient than they, putting on a great show of banter and repartee for the first few minutes of a session then drawing a line under that phase of the proceedings with a "Right, now let's get down to the work".

She might begin with the students involved in a boisterous word game:
• The pooling of derivations of local place names;
• A game of proverbs: one student leaves the room while proverb is selected and on his return tries to guess the

188

proverb by asking a question of each of his classmates who has been allocated a word of the proverb. They have to answer him in one sentence containing their word from the proverb;

•Synonyms round the class of, for example, the verb 'to walk' with students dropping out as they are unable to think of another one;

•Instant haiku round the class on The Thunderstorm (going on outside the window);

•A competition to see who can make the most four-letter words, reading any way, one letter contributed by each student in turn around the class, in a 4 x 4 grid:

The class is held this side of unruliness by a teacher who obviously enjoys them and expresses her enjoyment by bracing and vaudevillean orchestration of the event. Most will be happy enough to be swept along by the enthusiastic atmosphere; those who resist it might be seen as killjoys.

Once she has established this responsive ambience and her own influential position she can lead the session into a more sober stage.

Softly, Softly

Other teachers will hardly ever raise their voices above a whisper yet will make the most recalcitrant of students responsive. If misbehaviour occurs an intense expression of shock and surprise is composed and the miscreant is sometimes shamed into better behaviour.

The Power of Talk

There is a tiny minority of authoritarian teachers who dominate their students through threat and sarcasm, but they do not create conditions conducive to learning. Those teachers who form the vast majority, who like their students, who warm to their mischief-making and their idiosyncrasies and have a sympathy for them, would eschew punishment systems and would put their faith in

189

the power of talk. In the end the disenchanted student will only become a constructive influence and a learner in the classroom if he is persuaded of
• the teacher's good intentions;
• the value to him of the work;
• the worth of his own contribution.

None of these factors will he be convinced of except by the experience of the classroom and the consistent behaviour of the teacher.

With some students the talk will have to be ongoing and it might take many break and lunchtime meetings before any discernible change in behaviour is made; though a chance meeting in the town, a success on the sports field or the discovery of a shared interest can bring about a sudden breakthrough.

A Thematic Approach

Under normal circumstances it is, I believe, the teacher's responsibility to cope with the students that she has been allocated and to try by all her powers of persuasion or ingenuity to create a positive and diligent class. Severe indiscipline might be approached by setting up a full class theme on a subject such as Authority, Law and Order or The School, so that the issues that lie behind unco-operative behaviour and pertain to interpersonal co-operation can be examined. Such a theme is perfectly valid on an English curriculum and the discussions and activities might impinge on the awkward students, encouraging them to play a more constructive part. Work on a book like *Dr Lyward's Answer*, *Summerhill* or Mackenzie's *Out of the Classroom* will alert students to approaches to discipline that will counterpoint the teacher's own, and out of such debate could evolve a code of classroom behaviour agreed on by all the students.

A Direct Approach

Alternatively, bringing the issue into the open by extending a 'round' to a full class discussion about the problem could be tried: Here is our community of twenty-eight students and a teacher. We have a common aim and can only achieve it with the co-operation of all the members.
• What are the students who are presently making it impossible for the rest of us to enjoy reading, writing or

talking going to do about it?
- What is the problem?
- Why do they insist on being so anti-social?
- Do they understand the purpose and value of the present piece of work?
- Can we help?
- What would they prefer to do?

Student Exchange

If it is a group of disruptive students, each member might be placed in a different class so that the nuisances are separated; if just one, he could be swopped with a student from another teacher's class. In a mixed ability department this sort of exchange can be very easily effected. If the classes are set it can still be done, but it can be cruel if astudent of low ability is placed with much brighter ones. It has been known in these circumstances, though, for the students from the lower set to rise to the occasion and perform far above the teacher's expectations! But that is another story.

Orchestration

Indiscipline might begin to grow if many of the class have been working on optional work for a long time. When students are not used to exercising their choice they will find it very demanding to assume responsibility for their own work for very long. In many ways it is easier to acquiesce to the teacher's will and do her bidding.
In the early stages, then, optional work might be limited to periods of, say, three weeks and extended gradually as students grow more accustomed to its challenges. The teacher will need to judge when is the right time to draw the class together into a joint activity, a class novel or play, or shared work from a source book. The changeover should be made early rather than late so that students do not experience a period of ennui or fragmentation. There is no doubt that the students do need to feel that always in the background there is a competent, properly organised teacher. If the underlying structure to the systems in the classroom is perceived to be shaky or the procedures of preparation, planning or marking lax, then students will not be inclined to work hard themselves.

ay by Day

The teacher should try to

- be imaginative in the way she responds to her students and in her approach to her work;
- be consistent and reliable in the eyes of her students;
- be good-humoured;
- avoid confrontations and attempt to solve all disciplinary problems through talk based on a build-up of mutual understanding;
- be cheerful and interested, even on a black day;
- be in the classroom before the students arrive;
- have any home marking done as promptly and as sensitively as possible;
- whether it is the responsibility of the students or not, ensure that the classroom is always welcoming, attractive, stimulating;
- ensure that wall displays are never allowed to become tatty;
- ensure that the students feel it is their classroom;
- ensure that it is never too much trouble for the teacher to spend her time with them;
- ensure that, although there will always be a professional distance between the teacher and the student so that the relationship will not become possessive or intrusive, there will be a sympathy and a trust and there will be a proper concern for the students' social as well as educational well-being;
- ensure that, if she runs a file of ideas cards or an ideas box, she will keep this material up-to-date, replenishing it regularly;
- ensure that other resources will be kept properly running and art equipment will not be allowed to run down;
- ensure that other organisational aspects of the role of English teacher including theatre visits, the engagement of speakers or other visitors, the involvement of backup teachers like the curriculum support team, the poet-in-residence, the visiting storyteller, trainee teachers, the support teachers who will need to be fully supplied with lesson notes during any absence, the A-level English students who might have been enlisted to help in the tenth and eleventh year classes, are efficiently done;
- ensure that she is fully in control of her material, with the core syllabus planned and prepared precisely so that

one session moves seamlessly into the next and whatever is required for its delivery is at hand.

The teacher's job is remarkable for the continual, grinding pressure it imposes and if the organisational side is allowed to get at all out of hand it can become intolerable. Working sensitively and creatively with students day in and day out is extremely demanding, which makes reliable procedures essential, but it is very rewarding and fulfilling if the class and the classroom are efficiently managed.

A Working Classroom
Back in the Classroom

Here, back in the classroom, is the moment for which all of this has been a preparation, all the reading, the organisation, the building of atmosphere; and it is the students who seem to be doing most of the work. They are at their activities: writing in role on *The Loneliness of the Long Distance Runner*, preparing to write their science fiction stories, planning the role play about the shopkeeper, discussing *The Ballad of Charlotte Dymond*, writing a letter, a poem, a short story, and reading a novel.

Facilitating

For teachers unfamiliar with this way of working the worry is that they would be constantly rushing from one student to another, never able to satisfy the needs of any. This is not the way it works. The students will probably work best and gain most from the teacher's deliberate withholding of her help. She would be wise not to answer questions, not offer solutions, not give unsolicited advice but rather to leave the onus on the students to resolve their difficulties either on their own or in a group. Much of her expertise will be shown in the way she enables the students to find their own way, seeing every difficulty as an opportunity for them to learn.

So far this session she has held a 'round': everyone in the class knows what the others are doing. And she has worked with her core on *The Loneliness of the Long Distance Runner*. She has made sure that her directions on the follow-up work have been given very clearly and more than once and that she has talked to each of the fourteen briefly to ensure that all know what they should be doing.

The Students

She puts her head round the door of the small room; it is surprisingly peaceful in there. She asks if everything is all right and, after checking, goes over to the science fiction group where nothing seems to have been achieved. These students are finding it hard to start writing. They have decided on their material, have decided who's going to write what, so have made considerable progress, but they are unsure what a story for juniors really looks like. How is it different? The teacher thinks of stories by Valerie Carey and Graham Oakley and mentions neither. But out of the conversation that follows, the four students decide to fix up a visit to the junior school library down the road so that they can have a careful look at some children's books and talk to children there about their favourite stories. One goes to telephone the school secretary to arrange for a lunchtime visit while the other three discuss how they will proceed when they get to the school.

The *Charlotte Dymond* group has not progressed far with the dramatisation because the talk here has been to do with why Matthew killed Charlotte. The motive seems unnecessarily obscure. These students would like to make a video of the scene, which the teacher agrees to, but she asks if they can first walk through the early stages of the visit to the marshes to see if that is likely to increase their understanding.

With most of the individuals it is a matter of only a short conversation taking place.

The short story writer, having written a narrative told almost entirely in dialogue, has begun one which starts halfway through, so the conversation revolves around the effect of this feature of the story on the reader. The girl reading *The Haunting* discusses her reaction to the book so far, is asked to compare it with recent reads, and talks about where in her imagination she is when she reads a book: with the major character, with a female character with whom she feels sympathy, with the storyteller, or where?

The letter writer has finished but wants to check his format, so goes to the school library to borrow a formal letter from the librarian to use as a template. When he returns the teacher will work carefully with him, helping

194

him talk through the formalities of the language in this register and clarifying details of layout.

The poet is in the biggest bother. She has her theme but she doesn't feel that she is making any real progress with her writing. By far the longest conversation therefore takes place with her, the teacher asking her why she feels dissatisfied and what features of the poems she likes particularly appeal to her. Together they agree that she is writing too generally: there is no direct, specific experience in her poems. She needs to describe particulars from her own observation so that the reader can respond to actual events.

It is in the last two situations that the teacher might suggest alternative ways of organising words by using constructions like relative clauses and present participles. She works in the context of the student's own writing and by using examples from a private reader so that the student is led to recognise a wider syntactical range of options.

The Final 'Round'

At the end of the session the students will form a 'round' and tell each other what has been achieved. The boys who worked on the role play will perform their play and their insight will be shared by each student. This, to me, is the English classroom at its best: purposeful language use and through it personal growth. The teacher has handled the students and their work humanely, imaginatively, delicately. She has enabled her students to succeed and the achievements are theirs. By dint of her diligence, planning, organisation, knowledge and her personal skills she has made it possible for her students in their freedom to learn more about their language, themselves and each other.

CHAPTER SIX

TIME

It is important that students do not rush from one language activity to another in the classroom. To spend longer on making a response to a poem or shaping a piece of writing will result in an opportunity for deeper engagement with the subject and understanding of the resources of language. In this chapter approaches to poetry and redrafting are considered.

The Poem

As a teacher I used to issue a poem that the students might never have seen before and ask them to discuss it with no preparation time. I now believe that a poem should be given to the students some time before a discussion is held on it. In the intervening days the students could read it several times, think about it, perhaps chat a little about it, even learn all or part of it. It took William Jay Smith, the author of *American Primitive*, sixteen years of tinkering with his poem until he was satisfied it was as good as he could make it. I issued it one afternoon to my students who discussed it, somewhat; then I whisked it away again. I did no sort of justice to the poem and even less to the students, who must have felt that I didn't really value their personal response at all. As for the poem, it was the result of a profoundly imaginative act, and for us to get much of its deeper resonance would require the commitment of a great deal of time and emotional and intellectual energy.

Time and the Poem (1)

Patrick Dias is Director of the Centre for the Study and Teaching of Writing at McGill University, Montreal. He works with groups of five or six students to whom he reads a poem. A discussion of the 'meaning' of unfamiliar words follows, after which one and then another student reads the poem. The students are invited to pool their immediate responses, their feelings and perceptions. These are received without interruption or further comment, but some while later a general discussion ensues. Now the groups work in isolation, reporting back to the plenary class in turn so that an understanding is built of the poem cumulatively: one day group one will report back, the teacher doing no more than redirecting the group to the poem when necessary and redirecting questions put to him to the whole class; the next day, in the light of the previous group's comments, group two reports, and so on.

After two weeks of such activity the students are able to discuss with far more confidence than they exhibited at the beginning, and this leads to a more authoritative and, at the same time, a more exploratory mode of talk. The students learn to interact collaboratively and learn the techniques of listening to each other's insights or hypotheses, weighing them up, assimilating what they have been convinced of into their own interpretation. They learn a great deal more about how they might approach poetry in general, understanding more about the craft of writing, and they have in the process thoroughly absorbed a particular poem.

Time and the Poem (2)

William Washburn is Supervisor of Language Arts (English Education) for the Calgary Board of Education and the founder of the Calgary Writing Project (Canada). The experience that changed his style of teaching poetry involved him working one day with his students until their obvious boredom sent him out of the classroom in despair. Twenty minutes later he peered through the window expecting to see chaos but instead witnessed a discussion going on about the same poem on a far higher level than his own teacherly questions would have allowed. He developed an approach that has several distinct stages. He would select a 'difficult' poem, say William Empson's *Missing Dates*, and read it to the students, each of whom would have a copy. He would invite them to "make the most that you can out of the poem", at first on their own and then in groups without the teacher's intervention. He would then join each group asking how the discussion had gone. The group discussions without the teacher's presence had been taped and the next stage would be for the groups to play back what had transpired, stopping the tape whenever they wanted to add to what had gone before. This elaboration of the early discussion was also taped.

He found that this technique enabled students to move in the space of ten days from a state of virtually no understanding of the poem to one of deep and real appreciation. There would be a "great extension of meaning": the longer the students talked the deeper the understanding would become. After the first one or two discussions 'linguistic competence' would grow and examples and analogies would begin to move their understanding on.

He noticed, too, that his students' confidence in their ability to articulate a response, in validation of their understanding of the poem, was extremely fragile: the presence of a stranger or of a student who the rest felt knew more than they did, the presence even of a symbol of authority, like a dictionary, would block the flow of constructive talk. We generally perform orally less well under stressful conditions, and clearly part of the function of the teacher is to provide the most supportive context for learning that she can.

Time and the Poem (3)

I am sure that time is of the essence in the appreciation of a poem. The extract on *Green Man in the Garden* that is printed in Chapter One is taken from the end of an hour-long discussion. On several occasions the group of four students, who had been told that the discussion would be that length, reached a conclusion, looked at their watches, took a deep breath and got started again. Their conversation was a series of stages, with each stage screwing down deeper into the poem's centre as the poem became more familiar and as the students became easier in each other's company. This increased sense of ease seemed to allow them to focus more of their attention on their individual effort within the collaborative act of creating meaning and less on the self-conscious social side of their linguistic performance. They seemed more able to lose themselves in the experience of the poem, with the result that a deeper part of their minds was called into play. It was this interplay between the poet's creation and the deeper mind of the students that led them to an understanding that would not have been otherwise possible.

The idea of having groups of students working on the same poem and then meeting to compare their understanding seems a useful extension to the *Green Man*

198

in the Garden approach. The challenge of describing, elaborating and defending a point of view, comparing it with and coming to terms with another reading would help the students understand the poem more deeply.

Time and the Poem (4)

It is strange how our minds seem to stir poetry about over a period of time so that unsuspected and half-remembered flavours are released. It is partly for this reason that I think there is value in students learning poems by heart.

Learning by rote is generally the antithesis of learning through understanding, but the very act of learning poetry is part of the process of understanding it. The sound of a poem is an essential feature, and in learning a poem you need to pay particular attention to the rhythms and sounds which, once learned, become part of one's subliminal sense of the music and meaning of language. In learning, too, we have to relate to the surface meaning, to particular words, instantly memorable phrases and the syntactical links that pull them together; we become aware of the threads of imagery and sound that establish the thematic infrastructure as we do in a more deliberate way when performing a Tray exercise on the microcomputer.

And, once learned, the poem becomes part of our mental baggage to be remembered on appropriate, or apparently unrelated, occasions; with the result that our experiences have a sort of literary gloss to them.

Our lives are far richer for having a mind stocked with melodies, pop songs, famous paintings, photographs, buildings, nursery rhymes, proverbs. We use these memories to make mental comparisons, in discussions and for our own silent pleasure. Other verbal memories, phrases used by dear relations, telling lines from speechmakers' rhetoric, expressions that have a generic significance, whole verses from favourite songwriters, help make us the people that we are: we remember them because of who we were then and the remembrance helps make us what we are now. Why shouldn't the English teacher provide time for the learning of poetry for those students who want it?

It used to be my practice with a mixed ability class

199

when the students were all doing the same work to ask them to learn as much of a given poem as each was able in the allotted homework time (thirty minutes) and the next session we would discuss the poem in groups. To have got to know the poem through the attempted memorising did make it more likely that the discussions would penetrate deeper into the poem's meaning and that the familiarity would free the students to talk in a more homely way about it.

Moving on to more student choice I used to suggest that one option might be the learning of all or part of a poem either 'for its own sake' or as a stage in the slow exploration of a poem's meaning. An activity like the prepared choric reading of a poem would be more valuable if the participants had had time to get to know the poem better by memorising it. A dramatisation might be more manageable practically if the students were somewhat acquainted with the poem before the session began.

Time for Composition

We need to be careful when setting written assignments not to underestimate the amount of time a student might need to produce what to him is a satisfactory piece. I had an angry father at a parents' evening some time ago upbraiding me for the agonies I put his son through when I asked him to finish off a poem for homework. All I had known about the activity was that what he handed in the following day was of very high quality.

I had no idea of the torment I put this student through until my own son was required to compose a love sonnet during his half-hour homework. By midnight, after sweat and tears had been shed over the kitchen table and a few suggestions from Dad, fourteen lines of verse had been assembled that did not really satisfy son, Dad or, the next day, the teacher. Sometimes the assignments we set are too difficult to be satisfactorily completed and sometimes the time we allow for their completion is inadequate – sometimes, as with the latter example, both.

Time for Writing
Drafting

Some writers seem able to compose while having a bath or taking a walk in the garden so that by the time they sit at their desk they are ready with the polished version in their head; and some, with a literary gift, do seem able to bring such clarity of mind and focus of attention to the act of composition that they hardly need to alter what they first write down. Dylan Thomas could, at the drop of a hat, write an impressive verse on the back of a beer mat while sitting at the bar. But when he was working on a poem intended for publication his "sullen art" required several thorough-going redrafts, as existing records show.

Susan Price describes the torment that she has to go through as she struggles to find the right words and the right combination of words. But the results of her agonising are books for children of the quality of *The Ghost Drum*, winner of the Carnegie Medal in 1987. Writers vary one from another in their practice because of differences in temperament and facility. But no writer will be able to write to order invariably.

Depending on the subject, the time of the week, the state of the digestive system, one day writing might be a matter of comparative ease, the words flowing sweetly off the nib, and another all there is to show for a long struggle is a criss-cross of lines scratched across whole passages and a few arrows optimistically aimed from one part of a page to another.

Redrafting with the Teacher

The process of composition is different for each student too, and the ability to write well comes and goes; if everyone starts off together on the same written assignment some will reach what is to them a satisfactory conclusion long before others. Either some sort of extension work, or classroom strategies of the type described earlier, will have to be employed if all students are to be enabled to complete the piece to their satisfaction and if the nature of the writing process is to be allowed to influence classroom practice.

If we picture the classroom described in the last chapter and for Theresa we substitute Donna McMahon, we can consider the redrafting process at work as Donna and her teacher work together on the poem. Donna was able to produce her first draft without difficulty. This is shown overleaf.

201

My Street

I lay In bed Trembling
as I lay in my bed I hear Strange
noises. Whats that meow it
a cat calling for its friends.
Sounds crys cries of dogs
howling to get ~~free~~ free.
~~Engines~~ Engines of cars Tearing
down
Voices are street.
Morning comes creeping and
drunk and laughing
you hear birds sing all is calm and
quiet.

My Street

I lay In bed Trembling ~~at~~
~~as I lay in my bed I hear Strange~~ Morn
~~Noises~~. Whats ~~that~~
A cat calling for its friends.
~~Sounds~~ ~~crys~~ Cries of dogs
howling to get ~~free~~ free.
~~En~~ ~~gines~~ Engines of cars Tearing
down our are street.
Screaming Voices drunk and laughing
morning comes creeping ~~and~~
you ~~hear birds sing~~ all is calm and
quiet.

Broken fencing
Shadows
Dull grey buildings
Light shining on entry.

Shadows of the houses~~top~~
lie ~~too~~ upon ~~e~~ the grass.
The ~~foggy~~ sparkling ~~light~~ light shines ~~shining~~ on the dark entry.
waiting for something to Jump out.

---

lie
I ~~lay~~ in bed Trembling
Remembering the outside street.
The Broken fencing round the
nursery like a mad animal
Had ~~took~~ torn it to shreds
~~crs~~
The dull grey Building
gloomerly hanging
over The ~~go~~ glittering
path.

202

But she was not happy with this, so, with her teacher
helping her, she worked through three more drafts:

Second Draft (Stage One)

My Street

I lie in bed trembling remebering the out side street.
The broken fencing round the nursery like a mad animal had torn it to
shreads.
The dull grey buildings gloomerly hanging over the glittering path.
Shadows of the houses lie upon the grass.
The foggy light shines on the dark entry waiting for something to
jump out.
Whats that?
A cat calling for its friends.
Cries of dogs howling to get free.
Engines of cars tearing down our street.
Voices drunk and screaming
Morning comes creeping all is calm and quiet.
By Donna McMahon

My Street

remembering
I lie in bed trembling ~~remembering~~ the out side street.

The broken fencing round the nursery like a mad animal had torn it to shreds.
                                        from
The dull grey buildings. gloomily hanging over the glittering path.

Shadows of the houses lie upon the grass.

→ The foggy light shines on the dark entry waiting for something to
        pounce
jump out.

Whats that?
              wailing
A cat ~~calling~~ for its friends.

Cries of dogs howling to get free.

The Drilling
~~screaming~~ Engines of cars tearing down our street.
⚡ Voices drunk and ~~screaming~~ laughing
                                all is
Morning comes creeping all is calm ~~and~~ quiet.
        By Donna McMahon

                shines on
                ~~hanging over~~
The foggy light ~~shining on~~ the dark entry waits for
something to pounce out.

Third Draft (Stage One)

My ~~Street~~

I lie in bed trembling remembering the outside street.
The broken fencing round the nursery like a mad animal had torn it to shreds.
The dull grey buildings gloomily hanging over the glittering path.
Shadows of houses lie upon the grass.
The foggy light shining on the dark entry waits for Something to pounce

Whats that?
A cat wailing for its friends.
Cries of dogs howling to get free,
The drilling of cars tearing down our street.
Screaming ~~voices~~ voices drunk and laughing.
~~Morning comes creeping all is calm all is quiet~~

By Donna McMahon.

Morning comes creeping
(calm) and (quiet)

My Street

I lie in bed trembling remembering the out side street.
The broken fencing round the nursery like a mad animal had torn it to
shreds.
The dull grey buildings gloomily hanging over the glittering path.
Shadows of houses lie upon the grass.
The foggy light shining on the dark entry waits for something to pounce
out.

Whats that?
A cat wailing for its friends.
Cries of dogs howling to get free,
The drilling of cars tearing down our street.

Screaming voices drunk and laughing
Morning comes creeping all is calm all is quiet.

        By Donna McMahon

My Street

I lie in bed trembling remembering the out side street.
The broken fencing round the nursery like a mad animal had torn it to shreds.
The dull grey buildings gloomily hanging over the glittering path.
Shadows of houses lie upon the grass.
The foggy light shining on the dark entry waits for something to pounce.
Whats that?
A cat wailing for its friends.
Cries of dogs howling to get free.
The drilling of cars tearing down our street.
Screaming voices drunk and laughing.
Morning comes creeping calm and quiet.

By Donna McMahon

At times, according to her teacher, "the going was rough" as Donna worked on her poem. But by the time she had got to the fourth draft she was pleased with the result. There are teachers who feel that the teacher has intruded too far into Donna's creative world, so it is important to emphasise that Donna always felt that *My Street* was her poem. At no stage did she feel that her teacher had misappropriated it. Some teachers feel that the initial freshness of the first draft makes that the best poem; others are impressed by the way the nightmarish atmosphere is enhanced by the additional descriptions of lines two, three, four and five.

To me this particular debate misses the point. What is important is that Donna is left with a feeling of ownership of the poem, of pleasure in the collaborative and supportive activity with her teacher and of pride in the ultimate achievement.

Along the way she has learned a tremendous amount. One might argue that all the effort of scholarship, empirical wisdom and the drudge of day-to-day organisation, planning and preparation have led up to teacher-pupil interaction of this sort.

Because the teacher has a literary training, because she has learnt about interaction with young children and because of her understanding of the learning process she has been able to give Donna confidence to try more sophisticated expressions, to experiment with her imagery, to use her senses in a far more precise way; to express this complex and mysterious experience by contrasting 'the dull grey buildings gloomily hanging' with 'the glittering path', forming a sentence in which every word is made to work and catching the horror that lingers even when the night is over with the final line 'Morning comes creeping calm and quiet'.

Donna has created her own context for learning. Having learnt first of all by finding words to communicate her fear in an inventive and dramatic way, she was then able to work, with the encouragement of her teacher, towards a fuller expression. In the course of this five-day process she will have absorbed a great deal about what language can do, and the value of juxtaposition, sound, rhythm, contract, precise description and imagery.

She has also, it seems, learned a great deal more about the requirements of the reader, whose attention was claimed from the start by the question 'What's that?', and by the fourth draft is able to make much more sense of Donna's emotional state as a result of the descriptive passages. She has also corrected the surface features of spelling and punctuation: the final version will be read by others, so these conventions need to be tidied up. There is far more likelihood that Donna will learn the orthodox forms in what is a real situation, where the reason for accuracy is explicit, than as a consequence of decontextualised exercises.

It is when there is engagement like this that the real excitement of learning can be sensed. This is where the student comes into his own, and, therefore, it is where the teacher can be of most value. Everything comes together, the personality, the training, the experience of the teacher, to enable the student to improve his powers of expression. Donna will not have absorbed all that was covered in the progress towards draft four, but after this experience it is likely that she will be more confident and more competent in her use of language, in her reading and writing and in her oral work, and much more aware of the properties of language.

Redrafting with Other Students

Not that it has to be the teacher who acts as reader in the process of redrafting. Obviously at home and sometimes in the classroom the student will rework his writing on his own and some will find that in such solitary activity the necessary concentration can best be found. And situations can be set up where joint ventures lead to students in a group helping each other redraft so that not only are surface features corrected but more fundamental reshaping of the writing takes place. Some teachers set up groups of five or six students all employed in writing, and text is passed from one to another with comments added by each until it returns to the author, who responds by considering the comments and reworking his writing if he sees fit. This process can be repeated several times, and there might be some benefit to author and reader, but there is with this method a risk of frustration and tedium setting in unless there is a definite and appealing purpose behind the activity, as there would be in the children's story writing described in the last chapter.

Paired Redrafting

But the most simple and effective means of redrafting would seem to be where students work together in pairs on a piece of writing. It might be that both are working on the same sort of writing, but this is not necessary. What is important is that the writer has the opportunity in the course of composition to have the response of a reader so that he can hear whether his intentions are being realised and his communication succeeding. He will be able to work with the advantage of a colleague's critical response as well as his own, and it is likely that the collaboration of two minds will throw up issues and alternatives that might otherwise be missed and that will result in a productive session. The process of writing itself will have been a learning experience from which, initially, two students will have benefitted, and the finished product will have been improved.

Expressive Writing

Almost any kind of writing can become a context for developing a student's powers of expression and knowledge about the language through redrafting, as long as the student is thoroughly involved in its composition and keen to work at it. The student and student or student and teacher might work with a poem, or a passage of description, narrative or argument. Even an expressive piece of writing in which a student is trying to sort out his ideas for his own private satisfaction might be used, like the following, written by a Swindon student whose experience this was:

Dog Accident

On Saturday afternoon when me and my mum and sister were up at the shops at Cavendish Square a little dog got run over and all the people stopped and was looking at the dog and they stopped doing their there shopping me and my mum were among them and we was looking at the dog and all of a sudden this lady said you ought to be ashamed of yourselfs watching the poor dog at first the dog was in the middle of the road and then the man what knocked the dog put him by the kerb then a lady that new who the dog belonged to went and got the police and the dog was still alive the police did not phone the vet up and it took the police 10 minutes to get to Cavendish Square and they still didnt phone the vet the man what knocked the dog down had to get in a panda car then this man went and got something to put over it it was still alive it was only to keep the dog warmer than it was but the man got back and the dog was dead and the owners went and the lady owner was crying and we was sent away so we all went and everybody was saying the poor dog they could of got the vet for it before it died and it was still there at four o'clock.

As with *My Street*, any intervention by the teacher would have to be done with great tact because of the personal nature of the experience described.

A Different Audience

In this case the author has expressed a painful experience most successfully. His indignation informs the whole piece, which is detailed so clearly as to be a thorough re-enactment of the accident. It is an expressive piece of writing, done for the author's own sake, perhaps starting life as no more than a personal jotting, but because of his strength of feeling, his imaginative recall and his gift for storytelling, the jotting became a fuller exposition. The teacher might, therefore, invite the student to rewrite the account in a more formal manner, so that it becomes a more complete story suitable for an audience and therefore for publication. It might be reshaped into an article for the school newspaper or it might become the basis for a short story. The author might wish to write a formal letter of inquiry or complaint to the local police station or prepare a sequence of questions for an interview. If the student liked one of these suggestions the time would be ripe for a very worthwhile collaboration. The energy in the first draft would provide the impetus for a reworking.

With every piece of writing that is worth doing the author needs to feel that he has got it right, and whether the piece is right or not will always depend on its function. The writer of *Dog Accident* has clearly got it right

211

as a piece of expressive writing for himself. If he envisages it as a story for public consumption he will need to recognise the different purpose his writing now has and the different genre he is writing in and rework his material. If the writing is a transactional piece, an explanation of how a newly-designed board game should be played, a speech in defence of coarse fishing, a letter praising the parents of the local primary school for their efforts to keep it open, then it has not been 'got right' until the clarity, cogency, force of argument have been achieved to the best of the writer's ability.

Product

Some redrafting, then, requires a wholesale reworking in which the initial composition is radically reshaped. More often, if the author has been able to work with concentration, it will be a question of the substitution of the occasional word as the writing is in progress, the crossing out of a few lines that have failed to express what was intended or are redundant, a line here or there added on second thoughts.

Final Thoughts

•Sometimes a piece of writing will assume such importance in the student's eyes that time should be spent on it until a full expression has been achieved.
•Sometimes the material has found adequate expression in one form but so interests the student that his teacher might suggest he reshape it into a different form.
•Sometimes the needs of a real readership are such that time should be spent achieving accuracy of form and attractive presentation.
•Redrafting should be seen as a characteristic of the writing process. A writer will probably not set out with the intention of redrafting but dissatisfaction with the first attempt will usually lead to some redrafting.
•The teacher will probably enable students to redraft on their own, with the teacher, with another student and with groups of students, so that the benefits of these different situations can be experienced.

It will happen, then, that some pieces of writing will not be radically redrafted while other pieces that are more significant to the student will be worked on for some time, and during this time of self-criticism, reorganisation of material and creativity, the student's ability to handle his language will develop. He will learn more about the nature of the language and about his relationship to it. In producing fewer pieces of writing he will say and learn more.

The 'Round'
Negotiation

In the approaches to classroom management I have described, a great deal of time is devoted at the beginning of each session to the negotiation between students and teachers over what is to be done. This period of discussion and choice can be vitally important:

• It is good, in the first place, for orderliness: it gives a frame to the class.

• It is good for the exchange of information which enables each student to be kept informed of each other's programme of work.

• It is an exercise that can involve the whole personality, in determining the next stage of the next activity, in weighing up what has gone before, what current needs are, with whom one should work.

• In this time of real negotiation, active listening skills can be emphasised and developed, the listeners' attention being given to such things as body movement, gesture, timbre of voice, choice of vocabulary, eye contact and so on.

• To present the proposal cogently and persuasively, to discuss it purposefully, to modify the concept in the light of the teacher's qualifications and reservations: these are examples of the language being used to best advantage, in real and challenging circumstances. A great deal of English activity is taking place. The language is being used interactively so that a specific objective can be achieved, and if it cannot be entirely agreed to then a compromise has to be built and satisfaction has to be reached by both parties.

It is difficult to over-emphasise the significance of the learning going on here:

• Being a member of the class, a status which gives the student a compulsory entry into this 'round', he has to recognise the priorities and particular enthusiasms of his fellow members.

• He has to allow them time to make their claims and

argue their cases.

•He provides part of the audience which validates their speech.

•And underlying all these, the teacher is emphasising once again that it is the student who carries the real responsibility for his learning. He is the one who will decide finally on the book he intends to read and the nature of the response he will make to it. There will be guidance, at times strong; there will be suggestions and there will be tutoring, but in the end he will decide on the right book for a particular situation or need and the deepest, most subtle and most appropriate response of which he is capable at a given time.

Learning from Sharing Failure

When the 'round' is convened that draws the session to its close the students can be invited in turn by the teacher to tell the class what they have got out of the last hour's work. This is a time for the sharing of whatever students singly and in groups have learned. It is a time when the students themselves make explicit what has been achieved. There will have been failure, and it is the teacher's job to make failures a fairly rare occurrence; to be there to comfort, assess and rebuild when they do happen and show them to be a natural, even inevitable and necessary, feature of the learning process.

One of the most impressive sessions I have ever seen took place around a failed improvisation. The students had been working on it for some time and were in the process of putting scenes from the whole class dramatisation together when the recognition had to be faced that it was not going to work: the material was not strong enough, because it was not original enough, to sustain the drama. It had to be abandoned. At this point the teacher took a more prominent role, working through what had been achieved by the students, discussing with them the weak points and the strengths, helping them to recognise the major deficiencies and then, after a period of general gloom, began to build them up again. By the end of the session a more positive attitude had begun to reassert itself.

Failures like that are inevitable when creative work is going on, and all work in the English classroom should be

214

creative. Anyway, it was not really a failure at all: so much was learned out of what turned out to be only a temporary reverse.

Sharing of Progress

Of the students with work in progress, Theresa, or Donna, can tell her classmates what she has learned about the use of language from her experience of writing the poem. The girl writing the letter, the group working on science fiction stories, the group planning a video on *The Ballad of Charlotte Dymond* and the short story writer are able to pass on some information respectively about how formal letters are organised and the sort of language used, about how a small group works together to compose short stories on common subject matter for a specific readership, about the motivation of the murderer Matthew in the ballad and about the nature of suspense in narrative. All this perception is given to the class, not by the teacher or by just the clever members of the mixed ability class. It is given by every student, each in the process of creative English work. And the rest of the students, the listeners, are not going to stay quiet accepting this reportage willy-nilly. So a dialogue starts up after each account and perceptions are challenged, modified, elaborated on, deepened. The same process is gone through with the core members, who talk about where they have got to with their retelling of *The Loneliness of the Long Distance Runner* from the point of view and in the language of their character. Once more the class as a whole becomes involved in a discussion of the issues raised.

Presentations and Evaluation

Finally the improvisation about the Pakistani shopkeeper is presented. There is no ridicule of the actors' work because students are used to seeing their classmates in role in the drama studio and in the English classroom where role play is a frequent occurrence. They enjoy it and they know how much they learn from it. The play is performed and applauded. Because of the 'round' procedure, evaluation is seen as part of the session's activities, so the audience discusses what happened and how it was staged. Students, enouraged by the teacher, give their opinions and make their comparisons. In this case they are faced with the issue of racism and are able to tackle it from the useful distancing medium of the play, which in any case proposes a wonderfully obvious but luminous escape from intolerance.

This process of shared achievement and evaluation is so integral to the students' overall development that it should not be rushed. If more than one project is ready for presentation in the same session then one should be held over until next time rather than risk rushing the performance or the evaluation. In fact, this process of sharing and responding to students' finished work seems so important from a learning point of view that occasionally a whole session might be given over to it.

This last phase of the session allows the students to share their recent learning experience. The disparate activities are drawn into a communal activity. Tolerance of a more immediate sort is developed and maintained as each student relays his own work and relates to the work of the rest. The teacher tries to ensure that while the discussions on each piece of work are sharp they are also fair and supportive. The last phase moves through presentation, exploration, the making explicit of particular learning points and evaluation of what has been done to a time of reflection on one's own achievements and the achievements of others.

CHAPTER SEVEN

EVALUATING

This final chapter questions the usefulness of home marking and advocates instead discussion alongside the student in the act of composition or after a piece of work is finished. It deals with the vocabulary of evaluation and, keeping the student at the centre of the evaluation and monitoring process, it argues for a system of profiling that is based on description and includes commentary not only by the teacher but also the student and the student's parents.

Response
Proof Reading

For English teachers marking becomes a routine, an activity that takes place most evenings during the week and for a significant part of the weekend. If it is done promptly there is a pleasure, even an excitement, in keeping abreast of the work and maintaining some dialogue with students whose written product has been looked forward to. But the potential for dialogue is minimal and there are negative aspects to marking students' work at home:

•To mark a set of papers is extremely time-consuming for the English teacher, who needs to read every word and between the words.

•It is also very tiring. The pressure of marking night after night is debilitating.

•Marking every spelling and punctuation mistake would have a counter-productive effect on the student who made many mistakes.

•It is difficult for the teacher to set up a system that ensures that a response to her corrections is routine.

•If we are not extremely careful we mark as mistakes what are actually signs of the student's development as he gropes towards forms about which he has uncertain knowledge or application. If such tentative moves are marked wrong he might be less ambitious in future and his language development might be slowed down.

Giving a Mark

Although giving a mark or grade to a piece of work might be a useful monitoring system for the teacher (and is expected by many parents, governors and School Board members) it is hard to see how this practice can help the

217

student:

• A mark on its own might convey an improvement or a decline in the standard of work but it cannot reveal why it is better or worse.

• In a setted class there would, presumably, be almost no variation between students in the mark they achieved.

• If students are being marked against each other as opposed to against an external standard a degree of competition is being introduced which would detract from the intrinsic value of the work itself.

• In a mixed ability class the distribution would be a foregone conclusion. Students would tend to achieve the same mark time after time for their written work, which might demoralise the bottom students and make the top ones smug.

• The teacher would be habitually underlining her position as judge of the students' work. It would be hard for her to move from this role to provide students with other reader/audience roles.

• For GCSE it is the file as a whole that is assessed.

Perhaps the only really helpful addition by the teacher to a student's written work if the marking is done at home are the comments in the margin and at the end, which ought to be encouraging and positive, entering into dialogue with the student, emphasising the validity of the communication itself and sometimes indicating how the piece might be improved.

Alongside the Student

But this process could take place by the side of the student in the classroom while he is in the act of composition or just after he has finished. Then the discussion about the content of the piece could be genuinely two-way and the student's learning could grow as a consequence of insights he himself gains from

• questions put by the teacher;
• alternative ways of saying things that she might suggest;
• her treatment of his mistakes as learning points;
• their shared responses.

Spelling and Punctuation

On the simplest level the teacher can draw attention to the shapes of words that the writer is having difficulty with: that in English 'full' drops an 'l' when it is used as a

218

suffix; that the full stop goes there because that is where the longer stressing pause is needed. The teacher might ask the writer to read aloud and perhaps tape what he has written so that the force of her argument can be felt. He will then understand that for his own benefit and the benefit of other readers the conventions of punctuation should be adhered to: if they are, the meaning is clearer and the reading easier.

A Language Context

The student's writing is not taking place in isolation, of course. There will also be
• the work of his classmates, some of it on display around the classroom walls, some shared during a round and some written as a result of small group collaboration;
• the results of school surveys, investigative homeworks and fieldwork studies;
• work redrafted with the help of other students;
• the literature that is being read privately, in groups and as a class.

The teacher, interesting her classes in the geographical, historical and social variations and the grammatical conventions of spoken and written English, will make such dawning knowledge more explicit in the context of a student's own work so that more options become available to him.

Writer's Block

The writer might sometimes get 'stuck', unable to find the words or the constructions to articulate his subject any further. He has his models for writing in his head: what he has read of professional writers and his friends and what he has absorbed from talk. But he is unable to continue. The difficulty might be to do with the actual subject matter: he might not know what he thinks yet. In this situation the teacher might suggest that he
• tries out various formulae in rough, hoping that, by this means, he might get some fresh ideas going;
• researches the subject further;
• does some oral or written brainstorming;
• with one or two other students, sets up a small discussion group on the subject;
or she might
• by judicious questioning, help the student to a clearer

219

view of his position;
- generate alternatives through collaborative discussion.

Alternative Structures

If the problem has to do with the means of expressing a particular thought, feeling or experience, the teacher might use any of the above strategies, trying first to help the student by turning him back to his own resources and those of his classmates. But sometimes it might be useful to remind him of alternative constructions he might use, in the hope that this will help with the making of meaning.

As Douglas Barnes says in his essay entitled *Studying Communication or Studying Language*:
"It seems intuitively likely that some kinds of reflection and discussion of the details of language use does raise children's awareness and interest in their own and others' language behaviour and thus extend their abilities."

He goes on to say that:
"(At the simplest level this can be a matter of language games, and riddles, and play on words. Later it can become the informal but detailed examination of the range of texts, including non-literary speech and writing and the student's own productions, using methods derived from literary criticism)."

Word Games

Students will learn something about syntactical possibilities and stylistic considerations by playing warm-up games. Here are some examples:
- The teacher provides a list of three-word combinations:
  blue green yellow;
  blue green but;
  blue and not;
  blue and if;
  running fishing tennis;
  who when netball;
  though when blue;
and students, working in pairs, are asked to begin a sentence with each of the combinations. They cannot change the order of the words but they can use punctuation to create viable sentences.
- Each student around the class is asked to contribute a sentence to make a ghost story which is written on the

220

board. Copies are made on the word processor so that students, working in pairs, can improve the story's fluency by redrafting.

•Students are given a chopped up passage of prose or poetry and asked to reconstruct it, working in pairs.

•Students are asked to write a hundred words of prose without using any word more than once, or only using words that start with A or W.

The teacher can encourage students to put into words why some constructions are possible and some are not.

Starting Again

But it is by working to make his own meaning with the occasional explicit help from the teacher alongside him that the student will learn more about the structure of the language. And to be sometimes 'stuck' because the subject proves to be inappropriate, as happened with the drama group in Chapter Six, or the form or the treatment are leading nowhere, is in itself a most useful experience: learning about the language is going on in the struggle to find a way out.

Conferencing

Occasionally, the teacher can engage in the kind of interaction that Donald Graves, in his book *Writing: Teachers and Children at Work*, calls 'Conferencing'. Simply, the teacher has a conversation with the student on how satisfactorily the student feels he has completed his piece of writing:

•Is he pleased with it?

•Does he feel he has made any significant progress?

•What gave him most satisfaction?

•How does it compare with the last piece of the same sort?

•Has he learnt anything about the process or the use of writing through doing it?

Such questions will enable the student to keep hold of his work but at the same time look at it to some extent from outside. There will be questions and comments generated by each particular piece and in relation to each particular student, and the conversation should be a genuine dialogue, the tone interested, supportive and encouraging. The achievement should always be stressed and the conclusion should always be positive. The spelling, punctuation and handwriting should be considered and delicately worked on, but seen through to the communication beneath: because it is the communication – the expressing of the meaning – that should be the basis of the discussion. The concern should be to continue the process of helping the student gain confidence in the significance of his own experience and in his ability to articulate it, so that he steadily develops a communally-based independence and an individual means of expressing himself.

Evaluation
Self-Evaluation

Evaluation has been going on right through this process, of course, and it is most useful for the students when it is on their own ground.

• When the student is asked to compare the effectiveness of his recent work with the last piece in a similar mode he is having to call into play various criteria for judgement and the teacher will steadily be providing him with some of the terminology necessary to make a clearer statement.

• This ability to articulate judgements will be improved by the activity of the 'round' where his own work will be discussed by others and where he will be given a chance in turn to evaluate their work.

• Students' research work into the nature of language will be presented to the whole class from time to time.

• There will be literary criticism taking place, in groups and in the core, which will be fed into the whole class's experience during 'rounds'.

• The whole class will study texts together, during which time the insights of students and the teacher will be shared.

The insights gained into language use through these activities will be gradually absorbed by class members who will be able to bring them to bear on their own composition. The insights of one member of the class can be shared by all the class. The progress made in one aspect of language work can influence the whole field of language: advances in the techniques of writing will influence a student's oral performance and what is heard by the class as it evaluates a taped discussion will, over time and through repetition, impinge not only on the oral behaviour of more of the students but also on their

222

written work.

Explicit Description

A great deal of the most significant evaluation of the students' work, then, is done by themselves with the assistance of the teacher. It is part of the process of composition, reflection, composition. But the teacher has another vital part to play in the business of evaluation. How good a piece of work is can best be answered within the context of that student's own work and the student's own perception of his abilities, but even within this context the English teacher will need to be able to identify particular strengths and weaknesses not recognised by the student.

It is essential that the English teacher is aware of the deeper features of language and the areas in which development might be expected to occur, so that her response to written and spoken language use might be properly informed. The questions asked of the student about his work will be tempered by this knowledge, and at times there should be explicit reference made to help the student see the options available or focus on a particular feature.

Gut Reaction

Many teachers, when asked how they judge a piece of writing or a unit of talk, answer, with typical self-depreciation, that it is by impression, by a 'gut reaction'. But though it might be made without a conscious reference to a particular set of criteria there is a great deal of knowledge in operation in the background:
•The English expert will have a great deal of reading behind her.
•Through school and further education and afterwards there will have been novels and poems read, many of them discussed, at an academic or a social level.
•There will be a store of material that has been subjected to a more or less rigorous scrutiny with reference to several critical frameworks.
•This process continues with contemporary reading of literature.
•It continues with visits to the theatre.
•It continues with the viewing of television, when methods of evaluation are brought into play and built on.

223

• And this activity is taking place while in another sphere of life the teacher operates in the classroom, accumulating experiences of students at work generating language in all sorts of situations.

• The English teacher lives in a world of words. There are the books read for pure pleasure and there are the books – young adult fiction, for example – that are read in what is strictly speaking the line of duty, though the activity might still be a pleasurable one; and there is the language produced by the students. There are the department meetings and the consortium meetings when pieces of work are discussed and compared.

• There is staffroom debate about the merits and otherwise of students' work, and the shared excitement when a particularly successful language event occurs.

• There are the more formal set pieces when moderation or quality analysis takes place, when a meeting is held to look in close detail at three or four pieces of work or a transcript and tape of students talking.

• The occasional text book on the evaluation of language might be read by one or all of a department. New thoughts on educational matters have a mysterious tendency to become suddenly part of the atmosphere. Overnight they become part of teachers' consciousness as though handed down to each of us in our dreams by a good fairy or the Minister of State for Education. In fact they have struck a chord with the editors of the NATE magazine, found favour with the *Times Educational Supplement* or gained common currency on account of a memorable diagram or a good title. But, all the same, there is a need for text books on language development to be read from time to time, and the best place for the reading to become study is probably the department meeting.

**The Language of
Evaluation for Writing**

One of the most useful books on the evaluation of writing is *The Development of Writing Abilities 11-18* by J. Britton, T. Burgess, N. Martin, A. McLeod and H. Rosen. Another is Andrew Wilkinson's historical and critical account *Assessing Language Development*. His later longitudinal study of writing produced by children at different ages from the Queen Elizabeth Comprehensive

School in Crediton, Devon, describes in what areas and in what ways progress in writing occurs. It looks at the ways in which the whole person behind the writing is expressed through the writing and how the developmental processes of maturation and language acquisition become apparent. Out of this work have grown the more practical evaluations of John Dixon and Leslie Stratta who, with regard to the writing of narrative, for example, ask the following questions:

1. What kinds of ordering or re-ordering occur as the writer imaginatively recovers the events of the past? And to what effect?

2. Is the writer automatically assuming or taking for granted a reader who is already acquainted with the setting, or the characters, or the events?

3. Does the writer remain largely egocentric, or is there a more comprehensive perspective developing in which thoughts and feelings of other participants are more fully acknowledged or realised?

4. What actual or potential understanding of the uses of language could be pointed to as significant? In what ways is the writer beginning to move from a relatively restricted range of choices (in the use of vocabulary and structure), and to develop a sense of appropriate forms and tacit or conscious rhetorical strategies to evoke more complex textures of experiences?

These questions are exciting because
• they take for granted that the writer is on the move, is in the process of development as a writer;
• they have grown out of a meticulous and empathetic study of actual classroom work;
• they regard the writer as someone using the language interactively;
• there is a sense of the whole person growing behind the actual writing and of the reader, the recipient, with needs of his own;
• they are an implicit invitation for teachers to recognise the characteristics of writing and recognise, consequently, that we are in the business of description; of describing what the individual student as writer is up to.

Douglas Barnes, over the years, at first with Harold

Rosen and James Britton and later with Dorothy Barnes and Frankie Todd, has concentrated on the individual student's point of view, the importance of real communication and thus the need for evaluation of language activity to be descriptive. In *Communication and Learning in Small Groups* he and Frankie Todd set out an approach drawn from their own observation of students at work which takes into account social as well as linguistic moves in discussion.

The work of Gordon Wells might also be fed into department discussions, especially his longitudinal studies which set out, as did the studies of Andrew Wilkinson, to reveal the way in which students acquire and develop their language abilities. As well as the research he set in motion is the work going on in the University of East Anglia, where Terry Phillips is looking at small group talk, describing students' abilities in argument and the importance of role and context to talk. Strands from the work of the above educationalists can be seen in the research taking place in Devon where an attempt is being made to identify, through a description of students' talk, when learning is taking place and what is the importance of the task itself to learning through talk.

The National Projects on Writing and Oracy

Running alongside this work is the research of the National Projects on Writing and Oracy (NWP and NOP). For those authorities fortunate enough to be part of one or the other or both, the advantages are numerous. Their teachers are involved in a national movement; their work and the work of their students can assume a national relevance; they can become action-researchers, members of a team of experienced educationalists working together to learn more about how their students best learn to use their written and spoken language. But for those teachers not directly involved there are also considerable benefits, because they can read the descriptions of the research that appear in nationally available documentation and study the

•copies of students' written work;
•tapes and transcripts of students' oral work;
•videos of students' oral work;
•journals and diaries kept of their work by teachers and students

that are the product of routine classroom experience in the context of a carefully thought out English curriculum, under normal learning conditions, with the usual teacher and classmates. This is evidence of what students can do and how their language abilities develop. Teachers' commentaries take the form of descriptions of their classroom conditions and the characteristics of their students' writing and talking. The programmes of study are specific to each authority but relevant to teachers across the country. These are inspirational projects.

The Assessment of Performance Unit

In England and Wales the National Projects have been influenced by, and have in turn influenced, the Assessment of Performance Unit (APU) set up to monitor students' language achievements. Valuable insights have been gained by APU into the learning and evaluation processes and these have been published in its widely circulated magazines. APU has emphasised, for example, that

- if you have to give a language product a mark it should have an impression as well as a criterion-based component;
- assessment is more manageable and meaningful if made of specific language modes or functions;
- performance is task-specific;
- the quality of the communication itself is central;
- the language activity has to have meaning for the student if he is to perform well;
- context has an important bearing on performance.

APU's exemplar material and descriptions of students' language characteristics are a helpful guide to teachers' own classroom work. In Scotland, helpful insights have come from the feasibility study *The Assessment of Language*, sponsored by the SED.

The Scottish Situation

The argument in the ensuing sections relates to the specific requirements of GCSE and the National Curriculum in England and Wales. The Scottish situation differs in important ways.

In Scotland the Standard Grade assessment arrangements allow a considerable proportion of students' coursework to be taken into account. Teachers' estimates, based on two years of classroom observation, mediate grades gained in external tests of reading and writing. Talk grades are the responsibility of class teachers, whose assessments are moderated by teacher colleagues under the supervision of the Scottish Examination Board. Grade related criteria, in both summary and extended form, allow teachers to estimate what students are capable of and to place them on Credit, General or Foundation level. The separate grades attained for Talk, Reading and Writing are aggregated to a single, final award grade, but the candidate's certificate does give details of demonstrated ability in each individual mode. The grade related criteria are kept under continual review.

National testing in the Scottish context concentrates on attainment targets divided into five levels. Testing is carried out by teachers themselves, drawing on a national bank of test materials compiled by groups of practising teachers. Students are tested only at Year 4 and Year 7. Teachers in secondary school are therefore only affected in that they have an obligation to develop in an appropriate manner the language work generated by the primary phase targets. Level 5 represents the general standard of language competence expected of average students in Years 8 and 9 - Scottish S1 and S2.

National Curriculum Council

This, then, is the mainstream of evaluation of students' language work: led by the research of people like Britton, Barnes, Hourd, Dixon, Gardiner, Rosen, Wells and Wilkinson for whom the actual language of students at home and in the classroom was the starting point, and strengthened by the action-research of teachers in their schools.

And their work has informed the deliberations of the Cox Committee. The NCC's Attainment Targets for English and their attendant statements of attainment have proved a most useful aid to teachers in their articulation of their students' language development; and their usefulness is due in no small part to the unfavourable responses teachers themselves made to the *English from 5-16* Curriculum Matters document and the Kingman Report, and their involvement in the National Curriculum consultation process. The statements of attainment are well-conceived, detailed and, most important, descriptive. The Cox Committee recognised that language performance was idiosyncratic and task-specific. In other words, how well one performs with language is dependent on where and with whom the event takes place, how familiar or confident one is with the material, the form the expression should take, the conditions under which it is made and even such things as what the weather is like and what was eaten for breakfast. Achievement, then, could only be described with reference to a particular event, and could only be measured in terms of the success of the intended communication. The statements of attainment have helped many teachers know the language profiles of their individual students better than they did in the past and enabled many to focus their students' attention more keenly on details of their language work.

Schools Examining and Assessment Council

The organisation of statements of attainment into levels poses some problems for the teacher who also knows that her students' language development is a much more complex matter than such a structure implies. But she can continue to discourage rivalry and minimalist attitudes to education among her students, encourage collaborative learning and resist the use of aggregated scores with students, parents and colleagues, using instead description and examples of actual work.

Standard Attainment Tasks could damage the students' relationship with peers, his teacher and his subject: they are imposed on him, they have a particular status and their function is to test. But if they encourage students to work together, on real issues, and their work is evaluated by their teacher and themselves through negotiation, while it is in progress as well as when it is finished, Standard Attainment Tasks can become absorbed into their routine learning and provide a stimulus to student and teacher.

GCSE

In recognising that it is a range of work that grows naturally out of the classroom context that should be collected and that it is what the students 'can do' that should be assessed, the GCSE Boards made a remarkable

229

advance. They put the pressure of monitoring, collating and moderating on the teacher, but they offered a great deal of scope for the student to show what he is capable of and where his talents and interests lie, and to become involved in the selection and evaluation of his own work. It seems likely that in so doing they have rendered the examinations system, in which students in isolation produce unplanned, unworked, out of context, unreceived work, obsolete.

Moderation

Given the nature of language it is never possible to be categoric in ascribing a precise mark to one piece, let alone a folder of writing. A final decision should only be arrived at through negotiation between a teacher who knows that student's work intimately and another or others who are immersed at that time in the process of assessment and moderation. A process might be arrived at that has two elements to it:

• that schools should work in consortia, with teachers exchanging insights into the quality of students' language work; and

• that moderators from the Board come to the individual schools or to consortium meetings to view the students' work alongside teachers with whom discussion can take place.

But it is to be hoped that the Boards will eventually move to a system which relies not on grades but on descriptions of students' language skills, interests, habits and achievements; supported, where possible, with examples of their own work.

Monitoring
Mark Books

The teacher's monitoring system needs, above all, to be quick to do, clear and informative. She needs to be able to see at a glance if all her students are up-to-date with the required pieces of written work, if any of the pieces done are not up to the standard that she would expect and whether she has kept to her target with the number of oral assessments collected. If she allows a significant degree of student choice she will not have in her mark book columns for particular pieces of work and she will probably not be using a numerical or grading system for each piece. She might have her mark book laid out across a double page spread.

A tick could be entered in the appropriate column, a ring put around it if it were a disappointing piece or a plus sign put after an outstanding piece by a particular student. Oral marks would only be entered if they caught the student performing well.

One of the most important functions of this sort of cataloguing is simply to ensure that a certain number of pieces of work have been completed by the deadlines set. The teacher might feel that by half-term of the summer term she should have six English Language and six Literature entries and three oral assessments for every tenth year student. A glance at her mark book should show the current state of affairs.

To set early deadlines for GCSE is necessary because without them there will be several students in May of the eleventh year who have not met the requirements, by which time it is too late to avoid the unedifying business of a rapid production of relatively meaningless work, the antithesis of what GCSE should represent. I write from bitter experience. The sight of this writer fraught and speeding, driving round his school catchment area rounding up the last of his students' assignments was a not uncommon one at this time of the year!

GCSE Moderation

The horrors of this period cannot be avoided, but they can be alleviated if the department builds in a couple of strategically placed moderations during the course. There needs to be a programme of sessions throughout the five terms when teachers meet to discuss standards and compare their marking of particular pieces of writing and of videotaped conversations, but it might be useful too for there to be two longer periods of time, perhaps afternoons bought out of LEATGS or LFM money, when a number of files can be moderated. If one of these sessions were held in the second half of the summer term after the deadline for six completed pieces had been passed, a moderation could be held on files more than half completed. A second one might be held a month into the spring term of the eleventh year, when the files might contain the number of pieces required for the final moderation. To work in this systematic manner would establish evaluation and moderation as a continuous process and make the final operation less daunting.

The Book Book

The teacher might also use a 'book book' so that every student's reading programme can be monitored and books borrowed from the class library can be traced. An exercise book would suffice, one to each class, one page devoted to each student. This exercise book, like the mark book, would serve the interest of the teacher, so perhaps entries in it should be made by her rather than the students.

The Index

The student might have an index in his file which he would complete after every session. This would be his property, but the teacher would need to have ready access to it, indeed should sign it regularly, so that checks could be kept on the balance of activities engaged in by each student. This index could be kept inside the file's cover and be valuable as a record of work done. It could be used as a reference point in negotiations about intentions for future projects and might take this form:

DATE	ACTIVITY S/L, R, W	DESCRIPTION	COMMENT	CORE/ CHOICE	ALONE/ COLLAB.

In the activity column the student would simply write the initial of the main activity. In most sessions there would be more than one, probably a main and a subsidiary one, but rather than complicate the annotation unduly only the main activity need be entered. The final two columns would show how much time the student was spending on core activities and how much he was working on his own. If he wished to go into more detail about his reflections on his work he would use his journal. Of course the student could also devise his own way of recording his progress.

232

A Record of Achievement

A GCSE grade in English will say something about a candidate's ability to use the English language. It will reveal something about how well he can punctuate and spell and it will show something of his general ability to express himself in English. Although by the end of the course both teacher and student will share a great deal of detailed knowledge about his linguistic strengths and weaknesses, his interests, opinions, attitudes, sympathies and social achievements, none of this will be communicated by the grade he is given. By its nature English is not a subject that can be broken down into graded criteria, which means that a student's ability in this subject cannot be communicated by a single grade. We do not even learn from that grade whether or not the student actually has anything to say, whether he has experiences, ideas or feelings which he wishes or burns to communicate, or what specific means he has of framing that information.

A record of achievement that incorporates the National Curriculum statements of attainment can give a rounded picture of a student's language abilities, doing justice to the student himself and to the complexities of language. Some of the principles it would need to reflect are the following:

•Throughout the evaluating and recording process the student should be involved. It is his language that is being considered. During the formative and summative stages he has an essential contribution to make, and he will benefit greatly from the explicit discussions about his language development.

•The record of achievement should be formative, being filled in as part of routine classroom work, as well as summative.

•Information on the student's progress should cover at least the statements of attainment and include other features or significant language events felt to be important by the teacher and/or the student.

•The recording of the student's progress should be done through descriptive statements. These should tell the time and circumstances of the event and, in a brief statement signed by the teacher, describe the event itself.

•At the formative and summative stages the student's

233

parents should also be making their contribution to the language profile. These contributions could be made during parents' evening in meetings with the student and his English teacher or tutor.

• The student should at all times be encouraged to see this process as a positive acknowledgement of his achievements in the field of language.

• The descriptions of the student's language behaviour should be supported where possible by material kept in the file.

• Although the business of the levels will undoubtedly loom large, their somewhat arbitrary nature, revealed by the student's eccentric progress through them, should be emphasised by the teacher.

• The student's record of achievement, then, would describe precisely what the student did and could do in the field of language and under what circumstances. It would be the result of a collaboration between teacher, student and parents.

Learning

A fragile learner sits at the heart of the education system. He will not thrive if the processes of evaluation are not delicately managed. They should be part of the structure of his curriculum and intrinsic to his routine cleassroom experiences. They should, involving him throughout, describe his social and linguistic development in an informed and careful way. In these conditions, his confidence will grow and with it his ability to learn.

ACKNOWLEDGEMENTS

Page 68: *Dorset* by John Betjeman from *John Betjeman: Collected Poems*, reprinted by permission of John Murray (Publishers) Ltd. **Pages 77-78 and 176:** *Ma Faddon* and *The Fox Cape* by Heather Harrison, reprinted by permission of the author. **Page 106:** *Green Man in the Garden* by Charles Causley from *Collected Poems by Charles Causley*, published by Macmillan, reprinted by permission of David Higham Associates. **Pages 185-186:** *American Primitive* from *Poems by William Jay Smith*, reprinted by permission of the author. **Page 220:** extracts from *Studying Communication or Studying Language* by Douglas Barnes, from *Learning Me Your Language*, edited by M. Jones and A. West, reprinted by permission of Stanley Thornes (Publishers) Ltd.

Illustration: Julia King, Rachel Ward.

Much of the inspiration behind this book comes from the work of Kennet School English department. I would like to mention particularly the excellent classroom practice of David Cath, Chris England and Ian Parsons, examples from which I have used. I would also like to thank Jan Rafferty, now a teacher at Bosworth Wood Primary School, Solihull, for giving me permission to draw on her classroom work, and Donna MacMahon, who wrote *My Street* when she was one of Jan's students.
Thanks also to David Menzies for his advice on the Scottish perspective.